D0207796

The
Fanatics

By
Paul Laurence Dunbar

NEGRO UNIVERSITIES PRESS
NEW YORK

Originally published in 1901
by Dodd, Mead & Co., New York

Reprinted 1969 by
Negro Universities Press
A DIVISION OF GREENWOOD PUBLISHING CORP.
NEW YORK

SBN 8371-1264-8

TO MY FRIEND
EDWIN HENRY KEEN

Contents

vi CONTENTS

The Fanatics

CHAPTER I

LOVE AND POLITICS

THE warmth of the April sunshine had brought out the grass, and Mary Waters and Bob Van Doren trod it gleefully beneath their feet as they wended their way homeward from the outskirts of the town, where Mary had gone ostensibly to look for early spring blossoms and where Bob had followed her in quest of a pet setter that was not lost.

The little town was buzzing with excitement as the young people entered it, but they did not notice it, for a sweeter excitement was burning in their hearts.

Bob and Mary had been engaged for three months, a long time in those simple days in Ohio, where marriages were often affairs of a glance, a word and a parent's blessing. The parent's blessing in this case had been forthcoming too, for while the two widowed fathers could not agree politically, Stephen Van Doren being a staunch Democrat, and Bradford Waters as staunch a Republican, yet they had but one mind as to the welfare of their children.

They had loud and long discussions on the question of slavery and kindred subjects, but when it came to shaking hands over the union of Bob and Mary, they were as one. They had fallen out over the Missouri Compromise and quarrelled vigorously over the Fugitive Slave Law; but Stephen had told his son to go in and win, for there was not a better girl in the village than Mary, and Bradford had said "Yes" to Bob when he came.

On this day as the young people passed down Main street, oblivious of all save what was in their hearts, some people who stood on the outskirts of a crowd that was gathered about the courthouse snickered and nudged each other.

"Curious combination," old man Thorne said to his nearest neighbor, who was tiptoeing to get a glimpse into the middle of the circle.

"What's that?"

"Look a-there," and he pointed to the lovers who had passed on down the street.

"Geewhillikens," said the onlooker, "what a pity somebody didn't call their attention; wouldn't it 'a' been a contrast, though?"

"It would 'a' been worse than a contras'; it would 'a' been a broken engagement, an' perhaps a pair o' broken hearts. Well, of all fools, as the sayin' is, a ol fool is the worst."

"An' a Southern fool up North who has grown old in the South," said Johnson, who was somewhat of a curbstone politician.

"Oh, I don't know," said Thorne placidly, "different people has different ways o' thinkin'."

"But when you're in Rome, do as Rome does," returned Johnson.

"Most men carries their countries with them. The Dutchman comes over here, but he still eats his sauerkraut."

"Oh, plague take that. America for the Americans, I say, and Ohio for the Ohioans. Old Waters is right."

"How long you been here from York state?"

"Oh, that ain't in the question."

"Oh, certainly not. It's allus a matter o' whose ox is gored."

The matter within the circle which had awakened Mr. Johnson's sense of contrast was a hot debate which was just about terminating. Two old men, their hats off and their faces flushed, were holding forth in the midst of the crowd. One was Stephen Van Doren, and the other was Bradford Waters.

The former had come up from Virginia some-

time in the forties, and his ideas were still the
ideas of the old South.   He was a placid, gentle-
manly old man with a soldierly bearing and
courtly manners, but his opinions were most
decided, and he had made bitter enemies as well
as strong friends in the Ohio town.   The other
was the typical Yankee pioneer, thin, wiry and
excitable.   He was shouting now into his opponent's face, "Go back down South, go back to
Virginia, and preach those doctrines!"

"They've got sense enough to know them
down there.   It's only up here to gentlemen like
you that they need to be preached."

"You talk about secession, you, you!   I'd like
to see you build a fence unless the rails would all
stand together—one rail falling this way, and
another pulling that."

The crowd laughed.

"I'd like you to show me a hand where one
finger wasn't independent of another in an emergency."

"Build a fence," shouted Waters.

"Pick up a pin!" answered Van Doren.

"You're trying to ruin the whole country;
you're trying to stamp on the opinions that the
country has lived for and fought for and died
for—"

"Seven states have seceded, and I think in
some of those seven were men who lived and

fought and even died for their country. Yes,
sir, I tell you, Yankee as you are, to your face,
the South has done for this country what you
buying and selling, making and trading Yankees
have never done. You have made goods, but the
South has produced men." The old man was
warmed up.

"Men, men, we can equal any you bring."

"Calhoun!"

"Sumner!"

"Clay!"

"Webster!"

"We shall claim Douglass!"

"Lincoln!"

"I should have said the South produced gentlemen, not rail-splitters. We don't make states-
men of them."

"We produce men, and we'd make soldiers of
them if it was necessary."

"Well, it may be."

"Oh, no, it won't. Even the state that gave
birth to men like you, Stephen Van Doren,
wouldn't dare to raise its hand against the
Union."

"Wait and see."

"Wait and see! I don't need to wait and see.
I know."

"Bah, you're all alike, dreamers, dreamers,
dreamers."

"Dreamers, maybe, but my God, don't wake us!"

The crowd began to break as it saw that the argument was over, and the bystanders whispered and laughed among themselves at the vehemence of the two men.

"Wind-bags."

"Time wasted listening."

"War—pshaw!"

Just then a newsboy tore into the square shouting, "Paper, paper!" and every heart stood still with ominous dread at the next words, "Fort Sumter fired on!" The crowd stood still, and then with one accord, formed around the old men.

A slow smile covered Stephen Van Doren's lips as he stood facing Bradford Waters.

"Well, they've done it," he said.

"Yes," replied the other, wavering from the shock, "now what are you going to do about it?"

The old man straightened himself with sudden fire. He took off his hat and his thin white hair blew hither and thither in the cool spring breeze.

"I'll tell you what I'm going to do about it. I'll tell you what I'm going to do, when the call comes, I'm going down there and I'll help whip them out of their boots—and if they won't take me, I'll send a son. Now what are you going to do?

"Likewise."

Bradford Waters was known as a religious man, but now he turned and raising his hand to heaven said,

"God grant that we or our sons may meet where the right will win, you damned copperhead, you!"

In an instant Van Doren's fist shot out, but some one caught his arm. Waters sprang towards him, but was intercepted, and the two were borne away by different crowds, who were thunderstruck at the awful calamity which had fallen upon the nation.

The two old men sweated to be loosed upon each other, but they were forcibly taken to their homes.

Over the gate of the Waters' cottage, Bob Van Doren leaned, and Mary's hand was in his.

CHAPTER II

THE PARTING OF THE WAYS

" Don't you think a little cottage down by the river would be the best thing, Mary?" asked Bob.

"And then you'd be away from me every minute you could spare fishing. I know you, Bob Van Doren."

From the inside of the house Mary's brother Tom "twitted" the two unmercifully.

"I say there, Bob," he called, "you'd better let Mary come in and help about this supper. If you don't, there'll be a death when father comes home."

Mary's father was gentle with her, and this remark of her brother's was so obviously hyperbolic that she burst out laughing as she flung back, "Oh, I guess you've kept Nannie Woods from her work many a time, and there haven't been any deaths in that family yet."

"But there may be in this if Luke Sharples catches you sparking around Nannie," interposed Bob.

"Oh, I can attend to Luke any day."

"That's so, Luke isn't a very fast runner."

Tom threw a corncob out of the door and it struck Bob's hat and knocked it off. "There's an answer for you," he called.

They were still laughing and Mary's face was flushed with love and merriment when Bradford Waters came up and strode silently through the gateway.

"I must go in now," said Mary.

"So soon? Why it's hardly time to put the potatoes on yet."

"Suppose sometimes you should come home and find your supper not ready?"

"Oh, I wouldn't mind if you were there."

Just then Bradford Waters' voice floated angrily out to them,

"What's that young whelp hanging around my gate for?"

The girl turned pale, and her heart stood still, but the young man only laughed and shouted back, "What's the matter, Mr. Waters, you and father been at war again?"

"Yes, we've been at war, and soon we shall all be at war. Some of your dirty kinsmen have fired on Fort Sumter."

"What!"

"Yes, and there'll be hell for this day's work, you mark my words." The old man came to the

door again, and his son stood behind him, holding his arm. "Get away from my gate there.
Mary, come in the house. I've got better business for you than skylarking with copperheads."

The girl stood transfixed. "What is it, father,
what is it?" cried Tom.

"I tell you, those Southern devils have fired
on Fort Sumter, and it means war! Get away
from here, Bob Van Doren. There is a time
when men must separate on the ground of their
beliefs, and this house has no dealing with the
enemies of the Union, Mary."

But the girl's eyes were flashing, and her lips
compressed. "Go in, Mary," said Bob, and he
dropped her hand. His face was red and pale
by turns. She turned and went into the house,
and her lover left the gate and walked down the
street.

"Let this be the last time I catch you talking
with one of the Van Dorens. We are two families on opposite sides of a great question. We
can have no dealings, one with the other."

"But father, you gave Bob the right to love
me, and you can't take it back, you can't."

"I can take it back, and I will take it back.
I'd rather see you marry Nigger Ed, the town
crier, than to cross my blood with that Van
Doren breed. To-day, Stephen Van Doren rejoiced because his flag had been fired upon. The

flag he's living under, the flag that protects him
wherever he goes!"

"That wasn't Bob, father."

"Like father, like son," broke in Tom passionately.

"Why, Tom!" Mary turned her eyes, grief-
filled to overflowing upon her brother, "you
and he were such friends!"

"I have no friends who are not the friends of
my country. Since I know what I know, I
would not take Bob Van Doren's hand if he
were my brother."

"If he were Nannie Woods' brother?"

"Nannie Woods is a good loyal girl, and her
affections are placed on a loyal man. There is
no division there."

"Bob is right, Mary. We have come to the
parting of the ways. Those who hold with the
South must go with the South. Those who hold
with the North must stand by the flag. We are
all either Union men or we are rebels."

"But father, what of Vallandigham? You
have always said that he was a noble man."

"Vallandigham? Let me never hear his
name again! In this house it spells treason. I
can make some allowance for the Southerner,
living among his institutions and drawing his
life from them; but for the man who lives at
the North, represents Northern people and fills

his pockets with the coin which Northern hands
have worked for, for him, I have only contempt.
Such men hide like copperheads in the grass,
and sting when we least expect it. Weed them
out, I say, weed them out!"

The old man shook with the passion of his
feelings, and his face was ashen with anger.
There had been a time when Vallandigham was
his idol. He had gone against his party to help
vote him into Congress, and then——

It was a strangely silent meal to which the
three sat down that night. Tom was feverishly
anxious to be out for news, and Mary with tear-
stained face sat looking away into space. There
was a compression about her lips that gave her
countenance a wonderful similarity to her
father's. She could not eat, and she could not
talk, but her thoughts were busy with the events
that were going on about her. How she hated it
all—the strife, the turmoil, the bickerings and dis-
agreements. The Union, Confederacy, abolition,
slavery, the North, the South; one the upper,
the other, the lower millstone, and between
them, love and the women of the whole country.
Why could not they be let alone? Was there not
enough to be sacrificed that even the budding
flower of love must be brought too? It was
hard, too hard. She loved Bob Van Doren.
What did she care with which side he sympa-

thized? She loved Bob, not his politics. What had she to do with those black men down there in the South, it was none of her business? For her part, she only knew one black man and he was bad enough. Of course, Nigger Ed was funny. They all liked him and laughed at him, but he was not exemplary. He filled, with equal adaptability, the position of town crier and town drunkard. Really, if all his brethren were like him, they would be none the worse for having masters. Anyhow, her father had not been always so rigid, for he laughed when somebody stole the Bible from the colored folks' meeting-house, and wondered what they could do with a Bible anyhow.

Her reverie was broken by her brother's rising from the table.

"I'm going out to see what's going on," he announced.

"I'll walk up the street with you," said his father.

They took their hats and went out, and with a grey face, but set lips, the daughter went about her evening's work.

When they reached the courthouse a crowd was gathered there, and rumors and stories of all kinds were passing from lip to lip. Another crowd was gathered on the opposite side of the street, hooting and jeering, while now and then some self-appointed orator harangued it.   The assembly was composed of some of the worst elements of the town, reinforced by the young sports of some of the best families.   Altogether, it was a combination of hot blood and lawlessness.

An old friend of the Waters', who had been listening to the noisier crowd, brushed against the two men, and said under his breath, "Come on home, there's hell's work brewing here tonight."

"Then I'll stay and be in it," said the older man."

"There's nothing you can help about," replied the friend.   "You'd better come."

"No, we'll stay."

The lawless element, emboldened at the news of Sumter's disaster, determined to have some fun at the expense of their opponents.   With one accord, they surged towards the office of the *Republican*, armed with horns, and whistled, hooted and jeered themselves hoarse.

"This is child's play," said Bradford Waters to his son," if this is all they're going to do, we might as well go home."

They went back to the house, where for hours they could hear the horns and whistles of the crowd.

It was near midnight, when they were awakened by the clanging of a bell, and they heard Nigger Ed as he sped past the house, crying, "Fiah, fiah! De *'Publican* buildin' on fiah, tu'n out!"

The Waters were dressed and out of the house in a twinkling and had joined the crowd of men and boys who, with shouts and grunts, were tugging at the old hose-cart. Then they strained and tore their way to the *Republican* office where the fire had made terrible headway. The hose was turned on the building, and the pumps started. The flames crackled and the water hissed and like an echo there floated to the ears of the toiling men the cry of the rioters far away in another part of the town. They had done their work. It had, perhaps, come about unintentionally. They had only met to jeer; but finally some one threw a stone. The sound of crashing glass filled them with the spirit of destruction. A rioter cried, "Fire the damned shanty!" There were cries of "No! No!" but the cry had already been taken up, and a brand had been flung. Then madness seized them all and they battered and broke, smashed and tore, fired the place and fled singing with delirious joy.

The work of the firemen was of no avail, and in an hour the building and its contents were a confused mass of ashes, charred beams and molten metal.

When the Waters reached home, Mary, wide-eyed, white and shivering, sat up waiting for them. She hurried to give them each a cup of coffee, but asked no questions, though her hungry eyes craved the news. She sat and stared at them, as they eagerly drank.

Then her father turned to her. "Well," he said, "here's another sacrifice to the spirit of rebellion in the North. A man ruined, his property destroyed. They have burned the *Republican*, but they can't burn the principle it stood for, and the fire they lighted to-night will leave a flame in the heart of loyal citizens that will burn out every stock and stubble of secession, and disloyalty. Then woe to the copperheads who are hiding in the grass! When the flames have driven them out, we will trample on them, trample on them!" The old man rose and ground his heel into the floor.

Mary gave a cry, and shivering, covered her face with her hands.

CHAPTER III

PREPARATION

THERE were many other men in Dorbury no less stirred than was Bradford Waters over the events of the night, and the news from Charleston harbor. The next day saw meetings of the loyal citizens in every corner of the little town, which at last melted into one convention at the courthouse. Those who had no southern sympathies had been stung into action by the unwarranted rashness of the rioters, which brought the passions of the time so close to themselves.

The one question was asked on all sides: How soon would the president call for troops to put down this insurrection, and even as they asked it, the men were organizing, recruiting, drilling and forming companies to go to the front. The Light Guards, the local organization, donned their uniforms and paraded the streets. Already drums were heard on all sides, and the shrill cry of the fifes. In that portion of the town where lived a number of wealthy Southerners, there was the quiet and desolation of the grave.

Their doors were barred and their windows were shut. Even they could not have believed that it would come to this, but since it had come, it was too soon for them to readjust themselves to new conditions, too soon to go boldly over to the side of the South, or changing all their traditions, come out for the North and the Union, which in spite of all, they loved. So they kept silent, and the turmoil went on around them. The waves of excitement rolled to their very doors, receded and surged up again. Through their closed blinds, they heard the shouts of the men at the public meeting a few blocks away. They heard the tramping of feet as the forming companies moved up and down. The men knew that many of their employees were away, mingling with the crowds and that work was being neglected, but they kept to their rooms and to their meditations.

"Ah," said one, "it's a hard thing to make us choose between the old home and the old flag. We love both, which the better, God only knows."

The children came home from school and told how one of the teachers was preparing to go to war, and it brought the situation up to their very faces. Those were, indeed, terrible times when preceptors left their desks for the battle-field. But still their hearts cried within them, "What shall we do?"

In the afternoon of the day following the convention, Nannie Woods came over for a chat with Mary Waters. They were close friends, and as confidential as prospective sisters should be.

"Do you think they will fight?" asked Nannie.

"The South? Yes, they will fight, I am sure of it. They have already shown what is in them. Father and Tom think it will be easy to subdue them, but I feel, somehow, that it will be a long struggle."

"But we shall whip them," cried the other girl, her eyes flashing.

"I don't know, I don't know. I wish we didn't have to try."

"Why, Mary, are you afraid?"

"Oh, no, I'm not afraid, but there are those I love on both sides and in the coming contest, whichever wins, I shall have my share of sorrow."

"Whichever wins! Why you haven't a single friend in the South!"

"I have no friend in the South—now."

"Oh, you mean Rob Van Doren. Well, if he didn't think enough of me to be on my side, I'd send him about his business."

"A man who didn't have courage enough to hold to his own opinions wouldn't be the man I'd marry."

"A man who didn't have love enough to change his opinions to my side wouldn't be the man for me."

"Very well, Nannie, we can't agree."

"But we're not going to fall out, Mary," and Nannie threw her arms impulsively around her friend's neck. "But oh, I do long to see our boys march down there and show those rebels what we're made of. What do you think? Father says they claim that one of them can whip five Yankees, meaning us. Well, I'd like to see them try it."

"Spoken like a brave and loyal little woman," cried Tom, rushing in.

"Eavesdropping," said Nannie coquettishly, but Mary turned her sad eyes upon him.

"I am no less loyal than Nannie," she said, "and if the worst comes, I know where my allegiance lies, but—but—I wish it wasn't necessary, I wish it wasn't necessary to take sides."

"Never you mind, Mary, it's going to be all right. We'll whip them in a month or two."

"We!" cried Nannie. "Oh, Tom, you're never going?"

"Why, what should I be doing when men are at war?"

"But will there be war?"

"There is war. The South has fallen out of step and we shall have to whip them back into line. But it won't be long, two or three months at most, and then all will be quiet again. It may not even mean bloodshed. I think a display of armed force will be sufficient to quell them."

"God grant it may be so."

Tom turned and looked at his sister in an amused way. "Oh, you needn't be afraid, Mary, Bob Van Doren won't go. Copperheads only talk, they never fight, ha, ha."

"Tom Waters, that's mean of you," Nannie exclaimed, "and it's very little of you, for a day or two ago Bob was your friend." She held Mary closer as she spoke, but Tom Waters was imbued with the madness that was in the air.

"What," he burst out, "Bob Van Doren my friend! I have no friend except the friends of the Union, I tell you, and mark my words, when the others of us march away, you will find him skulking with the rest of his breed in the grass, where all snakes lie."

"Bob Van Doren is no coward," said Mary intensely, "and when the time comes, he will be found where his convictions lead, either boldly on the side of the Union or fighting for the cause which his honor chooses, you ——" She broke down and burst into tears.

"Oh, dry up, Mary," Tom said, with rough tenderness, "I didn't mean to hurt your feelings. Rob's a good enough fellow, but oh, I wish he was on our side. Don't cry, Mary, he's a first-rate fellow, and I—I'll be friends with him."

"Tom, you go away," cried Nannie, "you're just like all men, a great big, blundering—don't cry, Mary, don't cry. Mind your own business, Tom Waters, nobody wants you officiating around here, you've put your foot in it, and if you get smart, Mary and I will both turn rebel. Take your arm away."

"A pretty rebel you'd make."

"I'd make a better rebel than you would a soldier."

"All right, I'll show you," and the young man went out and slammed the door behind him.

"Now you've hurt his feelings," said Mary, suddenly drying her tears.

"I don't care, it was all your fault, Mary Waters." Then they wept in each other's arms because they were both so miserable.

Just then, the negro known as Nigger Ed, came running down the street. "Laws, have mussy on us, dey's hangin' Mistah V'landi'ham!"

The hearts of the two girls stood still with horror for the moment, and they clutched each other wildly, but the taint of Eve conquered, and they hurried to the door to get the news.

"Nigger Ed, Nigger Ed!" they called, and the colored man came breathlessly back to them.

"What did you say as you passed the house? They're hanging Mr. Vallandigham?"

"Yes'm, dey's hangin' him up by de co'thouse, a whole crowd o' men's a-hangin' him. Yo' fathah's 'mongst 'em, missy," he said turning to Mary.

"My father helping to hang Vallandigham! Oh, what are we coming to? Isn't it a terrible thing? Why, it's murder!"

Nannie called across to a friend who was passing on the other side of the street, "Oh, Mr. Smith, can it be true that they are hanging Vallandigham?"

The friend laughed. "Only in effigy," he said.

"Get along with you, Ed," said Nannie indignantly; "running around here scaring a body to death; they're only hanging him in effigy."

"Effigy, effigy, dat's whut dey said, but hit don't mek no diffunce how a man's hung, des so he's hung."

"Go along, you dunce, it's a stuffed Vallandigham they're hanging."

"Stuffed!" cried Ed, "I t'ought effigy meant his clothes. Lawd bless yo' soul, missy, an' me brekin' my naik runnin' f'om a stuffed co'pse. I reckon I 'larmed half de town," and Ed went on his way.

"And it's for those people our brothers and fathers are going to war?"

"Oh, no, not at all," said Nannie. "It's for the Union and against states' rights, and—and—everything like that."

"Those people are at the bottom of it all, I know it. I knew when that book by Mrs. Stowe came out. They're at the bottom of all this trouble. I wish they'd never been brought into this country."

"Why, how foolish you are, Mary, what on earth would the South have done without them? You don't suppose white people could work down in that hot country?"

"White people will work down in that hot country, and they will fight down there, and oh, my God, they will die down there!"

"Mary, you cry now at the least thing. I believe you're getting a touch of hysteria. If you say so, I'll burn some feathers under your nose."

"It isn't hysterics, Nannie, unless the whole spirit of the times is hysterical, but it is hard to see families that have known and loved each other for so long suddenly torn asunder by these dissensions."

"But the women folks needn't be separated. They can go on loving each other just the same."

"No, the women must and will follow their natural masters. It only remains for them to choose which shall be their masters, the men at home, or those whom they love outside."

"Well, with most of us that will be an easy matter, for our lovers and the folks at home agree—forgive me, Mary, I mean no reflection upon you, and I am so sorry."

"We are not all so fortunate, but however it comes, our women's hearts will bear the burdens. The men will get the glory and we shall have the grief."

"Hooray!" Tom's voice floated in from the street, and he swung in at the gate, singing gaily, his cap in his hand.

"Oh, what is it, Tom?" cried Nannie, "what's the news?"

"The bulletin says it is more than likely that the president will call for volunteers to-morrow, and I'm going to be the first lieutenant in the company, if the Light Guards go as a body."

"Oh, my poor brother!"

"Poor nothing, boom, boom, ta, ra, ra, boom, forward march!" And Tom tramped around the room in an excess of youthful enthusiasm. He was still parading, much to Nannie's pride and delight when his father entered and stood looking at him. His eyes were swollen and dark, and there were lines of pain about his mouth.

"Ah, Tom," he said presently, "there'll be something more than marching to do. I had expected to go along with you, but they tell me

I'm too old, and so I must be denied the honor of going to the front; but if you go, my son, I want your eyes to be open to the fact that you are going down there for no child's play. It will be full grown men's work. There will be uniforms and shining equipments, but there will be shot and shell as well. You go down there to make yourself a target for rebel bullets, and a mark for Southern fevers. There will be the screaming of fifes, but there will also be the whistling of shot. The flag that we love will float above you, but over all will hover the dark wings of death."

"Oh, father, father," cried Mary.

"It is a terrible business, daughter."

Tom had stood silent in the middle of the floor while his father was speaking, and now he drew up his shoulders and answered, "Don't be afraid of me, father, I understand it all. If I go to the war, I shall expect to meet and endure all that the war will bring, hardships, maybe worse. I'm not going for fun, and I don't think you'll ever have reason to be ashamed of me."

Mary flung herself on her father's breast and clung to him as if fearful that he also might be taken from her. But Nannie, with burning face, ran across and placed her hand in Tom's.

"That's right, Tom, and I'm not afraid for you." The young man put his hand tenderly upon the girl's head, and smiled down into her face.

"You're a brave little woman, Nannie," he said. The deep menace of the approaching contest seemed to have subdued them all.

"I'm not afraid for my son's honor," said Bradford Waters proudly, "but we must all remember that war brings more tears than smiles, and makes more widows than wives."

"We know that," said Nannie, "but we women will play our part at home, and be brave, won't we, Mary?"

The girl could not answer, but she raised her head from her father's shoulder and gripped her brother's hand tightly.

It was strange talk and a strange scene for these self-contained people who thought so little of their emotions; but their very fervor gave a melodramatic touch to all they did that at another time must have appeared ridiculous.

CHAPTER IV

SONS AND FATHERS

THE scenes that were taking place in Dorbury were not different from those that were being enacted over the whole country. While the North was thunderstruck at the turn matters had taken, there had yet been gathering there a political force which only needed this last act of effrontery to galvanize its intention into action. Everywhere, men were gathering themselves into companies, or like Dorbury, already had their Light Guards. Then like the sound of a deep bell in the midst of potential silence came the president's proclamation and the waiting hosts heard gladly. Lincoln's call for troops could hardly do more than was already done. Volunteering was but a word. In effect, thousands of men were ready, and the call meant only marching orders. The enthusiasm of the time was infectious. Old men were vying with youths in their haste and eagerness to offer their services to the country. As Bradford Waters had said, it was a time for sharp divisions, and men who had been

lukewarm in behalf of the Northern cause
before, now threw themselves heart and soul
into it.

This state of affairs effected Southern sympathizers in the North in two ways. It reduced the
less robust of spirit to silence and evasion. The
bolder and more decided ones were still also, but
between the silence of one and that of the other
was a vast difference of motive. One was the
conceding silence of fear ; the other was a sullen
repression that brooded and bided its time.

Among those who came out strongly on the
side of the South, was old Colonel Stewart, one
of the oldest citizens of the town. He had served
with distinction throughout the Mexican war, and
was the close friend of Vallandigham. He had
come of good old Virginia blood, and could not
and would not try to control his utterances. So
when the crisis came, his family, fearing the heat
and violence of the time, urged him to go South,
where his words and feelings would be more in
accordance with the views of his neighbors. But
he angrily refused.

"No," said he, "I will not run from them a
single step. I will stay here, and thrust the
truth of what I believe down their throats."

"But it will do no good," said his old wife
plaintively. "These people are as set in their beliefs as you are in yours, and you have no more

chance of turning them than of stemming the Ohio River."

" I am not here to stem the current. Let them go on with it and be swept to destruction by their own madness, but they shall not move me."

" All of your friends are keeping silent, colonel, although they feel as deeply as you do."

" All the more reason for him who feels and dares speak to speak."

" Then, too, you owe it to your family to leave this place. Your views make it hard for us, and they will make it worse as the trouble grows."

" I hope I have a family heroic enough to bear with me some of the burdens of the South."

His wife sighed hopelessly. It seemed a throwing of her words into empty air to talk to her husband. But Emily Stewart took up the cause. She had the subtlety of the newer generation, which in argument she substituted for her mother's simple directness.

" It seems to me, father," she said, " that you owe the most not to your family, but to yourself."

" What do you mean ? " he said, turning upon her.

" That if you are going to bear the burdens of the South, you should bear them not half-heartedly, but in full."

" Well, am I not ? "

"Let me explain. If trouble should come to the South, if disaster or defeat, it would be easy for you, for any man, to raise his voice in her behalf, while he, himself, rides out and beyond the stress of the storm. If you are on the side of the South, she has a right to demand your presence there; the strength of your personality thrown in with her strength."

The old man thought deeply, and then he said, "I believe you are right. Body as well as soul should be with the South now. Yes, we will go South. But I am sorry about Walter. He has been so bound up in his work. It will be a great disappointment for him to go away and leave it all. But then he may, in fact, I hope he will find consolation for whatever he loses in defending the birthplace of his father against the invasion of vandals."

The two women were silent. They were keener than the man. Women always are; and these knew or felt with a vividness that bordered on knowledge that Walter would not think as his father thought or go his father's way, and here the breach would come. But the colonel never once thought but that his son would enter heartily into all his plans and he prided himself upon the step he was about to take. His wife and daughter went out and left him anxiously awaiting Walter's coming.

They were apprehensive when they heard the young man's step in the hall, and afterwards heard him enter the library where the colonel always insisted that any matter of importance should be discussed.

Heroism, real or fancied, is its own reward, its own audience and its own applause. With continued thought upon the matter, Colonel Stewart's enthusiasm had reached the fever pitch from which he could admit but one view of it. He had bade the servant send his son to him as soon as he came in, and he was walking back and forth across the floor when he heard the young man's step. The old man paused and threw back his head with the spirited motion that was reminiscent of the days when he was a famous orator.

The boy, he was the colonel's only son, was not yet twenty-four—a handsome fellow, tall, well-made and as straight as an arrow. As they stood there facing each other, there was something very much alike in them. Age, experience, and contact with the world had hardened the lines about the old man's mouth, which as yet in the boy's, only indicated firmness.

"Sit down, Walter," said the colonel impressively, "I have something of importance to say to you; something that will probably change your whole life." His son had dropped into a

chair opposite to the one which his father had
taken. His face was white with the apprehen-
sion that would tug at his heart, but his eye was
steady and his lips firm.

Alexander Stewart could never quite forget
that for two sessions he had been a speaking
member of the Ohio legislature, and whenever he
had anything of importance to say, he returned
involuntarily to his forensic manner.

"Walter, my son," he began, "we have come
upon startling times. I have known all along
that this crisis would come, but I had not expected to see it in my day. It was inevitable
that the proud spirit of the South and the blind
arrogance of the North should some day clash.
The clash has now come, and with it, the time
for all strong men to take a decided stand. We
of the South "—the boy winced at the words—
"hold to our allegiance, though we have changed
our homes, and this is the time for us to show
our loyalty. The South has been insulted, her
oldest institutions derided, and her proudest
names dragged in the dust by men who might
have been their owners' overseers. But she does
not bear malice. She is not going to wage a
war of vengeance, but a holy war for truth, justice and right. I am going back home to help
her." The old man's own eloquence had brought
him to his feet in the middle of the floor, where

he stood, with eyes blazing. "Back home," he repeated, "and you, my son—" he held out his hand.

"Father," Walter also arose; his face was deadly pale. He did not take the proffered hand. His father gazed at him, first in amazement, then as the truth began to reach his mind, a livid flush overspread his face. His hand dropped at his side, and his fingers clenched.

"You," he half groaned, half growled between his teeth.

"Father, listen to me."

"There is but one thing I can listen to from you."

"You can never hear that. The North is my home. I was born here. I was brought up to revere the flag. You taught me that."

"But there is a reverence greater than that for any flag. There is a time when a flag loses its right to respect."

"You never talked to me of any such reverence or told me of any such time, and now I choose to stand by the home I know."

"This is not your home. Your home is the home of your family, and the blood in your veins is drawn from the best in the South."

"My blood was made by the streams and in the meadows; on the hills and in the valleys of Ohio, here, where I have played from babyhood, and father, I can't—I can't. May we not think differently and be friends?"

"No, if you had the blood of a single Yankee ancestor in you, I would impute it to that and forgive the defection; I could understand your weakening at this time, but——"

"It is not weakening," Walter flashed back, "if anything, it is strengthening when a man stands up for his flag, for the only flag he has ever known, when it is attacked by traitors."

"Traitors!" the old man almost shouted the word as he made a step towards the boy.

"Traitors, yes, traitors," said the son, unflinchingly.

"You cur, you mongrel cur, neither Northern nor Southern!"

"Father——"

"Silence! I wish the North joy of your acquisition. The South is well shed of you. You would have been like to turn tail and skulked in her direst extremity. It is well to know what you are from the start."

"Let me say a word, father."

"Don't father me. I'll father no such weak-kneed renegade as you are. From to-day, you are no son of mine. I curse you—curse you!"

The door opened softly and Mrs. Stewart stood there, transfixed, gazing at the two men. She was very pale for she had heard the last words.

"Husband, Walter —" she said tremulously, "I have intruded, but I could not help it."

Neither man spoke.

"Alexander," she went on, "take back those words. I felt all along it would be so, but you and Walter can disagree with each other and yet be father and son. Walter, come and shake hands with your father." The boy took a reluctant step forward, without raising his head, but his father drew himself up and folded his arms.

"Alexander!"

"I have no son," he said simply.

Walter raised his eyes and answered, "And I no father," and seizing his mother in his arms, he covered her face with kisses, and rushed from the room. Presently they heard the front door close behind him.

"Call him back, husband, call him back, for God's sake. He is our son, the only one left—call him back!"

The colonel stood like a statue. Not a muscle of his face quivered, and his folded arms were like iron in their tenseness. "He has chosen his faith," he said. He relaxed then to receive his wife's fainting form in his arms. He laid her gently on a couch and calling his daughter and the servants, went to his own room.

It is an awful thing to have to answer to a

mother for her boy. To see her eyes searching your soul with the question in them, "Where is my child?" But it is a more terrible thing to a father's conscience when he himself is questioner, accuser and culprit in one. Colonel Stewart walked his room alone and thought with agony over his position. He knew Walter's disposition. It was very like his own, and this was not a matter in which to say, "I have been hasty," and then allow it to pass over. How could he meet his wife's accusing eyes? How could he do without Walter? The old man sat down and buried his face in his hands. The fire and enthusiasm of indignation which had held him up during his interview with his son had left him, and he was only a sad, broken old man. If he could but stay in his room forever, away from everybody.

As soon as his wife recovered from her swoon she sent for him. He went tremblingly and reluctantly to her, fearful of what he should see in her eyes. The room, though, was sympathetically darkened when he went in. He groped his way to the bed. A hand reached out and took his and a voice said, "Let us hurry, let us go away from here, Alexander." There was no anger, no reproach in the tone, only a deep, lingering sadness that tore at his heartstrings.

"Margaret, Margaret!" he cried, and flinging

his arms about her, held her close while sobs shook his frame.

His wife patted his grey hair. "Don't cry, beloved," she said, "this is war. But let us go away from here. Let us go away."

"Yes, Margaret," he sobbed, "we will go away."

Preparations for the departure of the Stewarts began immediately. Mrs. Stewart busied herself feverishly as one who works to drive out bitter thoughts. But the colonel kept to his room away from the scenes of activity. His trouble weighed heavily upon him. His enthusiasm for the war seemed suddenly to have turned its heat malignantly upon him to consume him. Except when circumstances demanded his presence, he kept away from the rest of the family, no longer through the mere dread of meeting them, for it was the spirit of his conscience to press the iron into his soul; but because he felt that this was a trouble to be borne alone. No one could share it, no one could understand it.

For several days no one outside of the house knew of the breach that had occurred in the Stewart family, nor of their intention to go South. Then they made the mistake of hiring the negro, Ed, to help them finish their packing.

The servant is always curious; the negro

servant particularly so, and to the negro the very atmosphere of this silent house, the constrained attitude of the family were pregnant with mystery. Then he did not see the son about. It took but a little time for his curiosity to lead to the discovery that the son was boarding in the town. This, with scraps of information got from the other servants, he put together, and his imagination did the rest. Ed had a picturesque knack for lying, and the tale that resulted from his speculations was a fabric worthy of its weaver.

According to the negro's version, the colonel, though long past the age for service, was going down South to be a general, and wanted to take his son, Walter, along with him to be a captain. Walter had refused, and he and his father had come to fisticuffs in which the young man was worsted, for Ed added admiringly by way of embellishment, "Do ol' cunnel is a mighty good man yit." After this the young man had left his father's house because he thought he was too old to be whipped.

This was the tale with which Ed regaled the people for whom he worked about Dorbury; but be it said in vindication of their common sense that few, if any, believed it. That there was some color of fact in the matter they could not doubt when it was plainly shown that

Walter Stewart was not living at his father's house. There must have been a breach of some kind, they admitted, but Ed's picture must be reduced about one-half.

The story, however, threw young Stewart into an unenviable prominence. As modest as it is natural for a young man of twenty-three to be, it gave him no pleasure to have people turn around to look after him with an audible, "There he goes!"

At first, his feeling towards his father had been one, not so much of anger as of grief. But he had no confidant, and the grief that could not find an outlet hardened into a grief that sticks in the throat, that cannot be floated off by tears or blown away by curses that will not melt, that will not move, that becomes rebellion. It was all unjust. He thought of the ideas of independence that his father had inculcated in him; how he had held up to him the very strength of manhood which he now repudiated. How he had set before him the very example upon which he now modeled his conduct, and then abased it. He had built and broken his own idol, and the ruins lay not only about his feet, but about his son's. It was a hard thought in the boy's mind, and for a time he felt as if he wanted to hold his way in the world, asking of nothing, is it right or wrong? leaning to no beliefs, following no principles. This was the first mad rebellion of his flowering youth against the fading ideals, against the revelation of things as they are. But with the rebound, which marks the dividing line between youth and manhood, he came back to a saner view of the affair.

It came to him for the first time that now was a period of general madness in which no rule of sane action held good. And yet, he could not wholly forgive his father his unnecessary harshness. The understanding of his unmerited cruelty came to him, but his condemnation of it did not leave. Only once did he ask himself whether the cause for which he stood was worthy of all that he had sacrificed for it; home, mother, comfort and a father's love. Then there came back to him the words his father had uttered on a memorable occasion, "Walter, principle is too dear to be sacrificed at any price," and his lips closed in a line of determination. Resolutely he turned his face away from that path of soft delight. He was no longer his father's son; but he was enough of a Stewart to believe strongly.

He felt sorely hurt, though, when he found that Ed's story, while failing to find a resting-place in the ears of the sensible, had percolated the minds of the lower classes of the town. He heard ominous threats hurled at the old copperhead, which he knew to be directed at his father. All that lay in his power to do, he did to stem the tide of popular anger, but he felt it rising steadily, and knew that at any moment it might take the form of open violence or insult to his family. This must be avoided, he determined, and night after night, after he had left home, he patrolled the sidewalk in front of his father's house, and the grief-stricken mother, reaching out her arms and moaning for her son in her sleep, did not know that he was there, watching the low flicker of the night lamp in her room.

It was nearly a week after the memorable evening interview between Walter and his father that the young man received by the hands of the gossiping Ed a note from his mother. It ran, "We expect to go to-morrow evening at seven. Will you not come and tell me good-bye?" Walter was brave, and he gulped hard. This was from his mother, and neither principle nor anything else separated him from her. He would go. He wrote, "I will come in by the side gate, and wait for you in the arbor."

The evening found him there a half hour before the time set, but a mother's fond eagerness had outrun the hours and Mrs. Stewart was already there awaiting him. She embraced her son with tears in her eyes, and they talked long together. From the window of his room, Colonel

Stewart watched them. His eyes lingered over every outline of his son's figure. Once, he placed his hand on the sash as if to raise it. Then he checked himself and took a turn round the dismantled room. When he came back to the window, Walter was taking his leave. The old man saw his wife clinging about the boy's neck. He saw the young fellow brush his hand hastily across his eyes. Again, his hand went out involuntarily to the window, but he drew it back and ground it in the other while a groan struggled up from under the weight of his pride and tore itself from his pale lips. Gone, gone, Walter was gone, and with him, his chance of reconciliation. He saw his wife return, but he locked his door and sat down to battle with his pride and grief until it was time to go.

It was a worn-looking old man that came down to step into the carriage an hour later. But Colonel Stewart never looked more the soldier. Walter was at a safe point of vantage, watching to get a last glimpse of his family. He was heavy of heart in spite of his bravery. But suddenly, his sadness flamed into anger. A crowd had been gathering about his father's house, but he thought it only the usual throng attracted by curiosity. As his father stepped into the carriage, he heard a sudden huzza. The people had surrounded the vehicle. A band appeared, and there floated to his ears the strains of the Rogues' march. A red mist came before his eyes, but through it he could not help seeing that they were taking the horses from the shafts. He waited to see no more, but dashed down the street. He forgot his sorrow, he forgot the breach, he forgot everything but his fury. It was his father; his father.

They were drawing the carriage toward him now, and the band was crashing out the hateful music. He reached the crowd and dashed into it like a young bull, knocking the surprised rioters and musicians right and left. He was cursing; he was pale, and his lip was bleeding where he had bitten it. The music stopped. Those who held the shafts dropped them. They were too astonished by the sudden onslaught to move. Then a growl rose like the noise of wild beasts and the crowd began to surge upon the young man. Forward and back they swept him, struggling and fighting. Then the carriage door opened and Colonel Stewart stepped out. His face was the face of an angel in anger, or perhaps of a very noble devil.

"Stop," he thundered, and at his voice, the uproar ceased. "Take up the shafts, my fellow-citizens," he said sneeringly, "this act is what I might have expected of you, but go on. It is meet that I should be drawn by such cattle."

Then turning to his son, he said, "Sir, I need no defence from you." There was a joyous cry at this, though it was the young man's salvation. Some one hurled a stone, which grazed the old man's head. Walter was at the coward's side in an instant, and had felled him to the ground. For an instant, something that was not contempt gleamed in the old man's eye, but Walter turned, and lifting his hat to his father, backed from the crowd. They took up the shafts again. The musicians gathered their courage, and with a shout they bore the colonel away to the station.

Walter stood looking after the carriage. He had caught a glimpse of his mother's face from the window for a moment, and to the day of his death he never forgot the look she gave him. It was to be a help to him in the time of his trouble, and strength when the fight was hottest. His anger at his father had melted away in the flash of action. But he could not help wonder if the colonel's insult to him had been sincere, or only for the purpose of accomplishing what it did, the diversion of the crowd. He knew that he had been saved rough handling, and that his father had saved him, and he went home with a calmer spirit than he had known for many days.

Despite the intolerance which kept Stephen

Van Doren always at loggerheads with Bradford Waters, he was in reality a fairly reasonable man. He was as deep and ardent a partisan of the South as Colonel Stewart, and if he was not less anxious that his son should espouse her cause, at least he had more patience, and more faith to wait for his boy to turn to the right path.

From the time that Robert Van Doren was driven from his sweetheart's gate, there had been a silence between father and son as to the latter's intentions. But as the feverish preparations went on, Stephen Van Doren grew more and more uneasy and excited. It was hard not to speak to his son and find out from him where he stood in regard to the questions which were agitating his fellows. But a stalwart pride held the old man back. There were times when he told himself that the boy only waited for a word from him. But that word he determined never to say. The South did not need the arm of any one who had to be urged to fight for her.

The struggle and anxiety which possessed his father's mind was not lost on the young man, and he sympathized with the trouble, while he respected the fine courtly breeding which compelled silence under it. As for himself, he must have more time to think. This was no light question which he was now called upon to decide.

The times were asking of every American in his position, "Are you an American or a Southerner first?" The answer did not hang ready upon his lips. Where foes from without assailed, it was the country, the whole country. Could there arise any internal conditions that would make it different?

Finally, he could not stand the pained question in his father's eyes any longer. A word would let him know that, at least, his son was thinking of the matter which agitated him.

"Father," he said, "you are worrying about me."

The old man looked up proudly, "You are mistaken," was the reply, "I have no need to worry about my son. He is a man."

Robert gave his father a grateful glance, and went on, "You are right, you need not worry. I am looking for the right. When I find it, you may depend upon me to go that way."

"I am sure of it, Bob!" exclaimed the old man, grasping his son's hand, "I am sure you will. You are a man and must judge for yourself. I have confidence in you, Bob."

"Thank you, father."

They pressed each other's hands warmly, the cloud cleared from Van Doren's brow and the subject was dropped between the two.

Between Tom Waters and his father from the very first, there had been only harmony. There was a brief period of silence between them when Bradford Waters first fully realized that his age put him hopelessly beyond the chance of being beside his son in the ranks. At the first intimation that he was too old, he had scouted the idea, and said that it often took a grey head to manage a strong arm rightly. But when he saw the full quota of militia made up and his application denied, it filled him with poignant grief.

"I had so hoped to be by your side, Tom, in this fight," he said.

"It's best, father, as it is, though, for there's Mary to be taken care of."

"Yes, the fever in our blood makes us forget the nearest and dearest nowadays, but I'm glad that you will be there to represent me anyway."

From that time all the enthusiasm which Waters had felt in the Northern cause was centred upon his son. He watched him on the parade ground with undisguised pride, and when Tom came home in the glory of his new uniform, with the straps upon his square shoulders, Bradford Waters' voice was husky, and there was a moisture in his eyes as he said, " I'm glad now that it's you who are going, Tom, for I understand what a poor figure I must have made among you young fellows."

The son was too joyous to be much affected by the sadness in his father's tone, and he only laughed as he replied, " I tell you, father, those steel muscles of yours would have put many a young fellow to the blush when it came to endurance."

" Well, it isn't my chance. You're the soldier."

The young fellow would have felt a pardonable pride could he have known that his father was saying over and over again, " Lieutenant Thomas Waters, Lieutenant Thomas Waters, why not captain or colonel ? " And his pride would have been tempered could he have known also that back of this exclamation was the question, " Will he come back to me ? "

For so long a time had Bradford Waters been both father and mother to his son that he had come to have some of the qualities of both parents. And if it were true, as Mary said, that in this war the women's hearts would suffer most, then must he suffer doubly. With the woman's heart of the mother and the man's heart of the father, the ache had already begun for the struggle was on between the tenderness of the one and the pride of the other ; between the mother's love and the father's ambition. At the barracks, or on the parade ground, in the blare of the trumpets where Lieutenant Waters strode back and forth, ambition conquered. But in the long still nights when his boy Tom was in his thoughts and dreams, only love and tenderness held him.

CHAPTER V

"THE POMP AND CIRCUMSTANCE"

THE shifting scenes in the panorama of the opening war brought about the day of departure. The company to which Tom Waters belonged was to leave on an afternoon train for Columbus, and Dorbury was alert to see them off; friend and foe swayed by the same excitement. The town took on the appearance and spirit of a gala day. The streets were full of sight-seers, pedestrians, riders and drivers, for the event had brought in the farmers from surrounding townships. Here and there, the blue of a uniform showed among the crowd and some soldier made his way proudly, the centre of an admiring crowd. A troop of little boys fired by the enthusiasm of their elders marched to and fro to the doubtful tune of a shrill fife and an asthmatic drum. People who lived a long distance away, and who consequently had been compelled to start long before sunrise, now lolled lazily around, munching ginger-bread, or sat more decorously in the public square, eating their delayed breakfasts.

About the barracks, which were the quarters of the militia, was gathered a heterogeneous crowd. Within, there was the sound of steady tramping, as the sentinels moved back and forth over their beats. Their brothers without, were doing a more practical duty, for it took all the bravery of their bristling bayonets to keep back the curious. There was a stir among them like the rippling of the sea by the wind when a young man in the uniform of a private of the Light Guards hastened up and elbowed his way towards the door. There was a buzz, a single shout, and then a burst of cheers, as the young man, flushed and hot, leaped up the steps and entered the door. Some who had been his enemies were in the crowd; some who had laid violent hands on him only a few days before, but they were all his friends now. It was Walter Stewart. He had followed the leadings of his own mind and stayed with his company; but somehow the applause of these people who were all his father's enemies, was very bitter to him.

After Stewart, came a figure that elicited a shout from the throng, and a burst of laughter. It was the town crier, Negro Ed, who was to go as servant to the militia captain, Horace Miller.

"Hi, Ed," called one, "ain't you afraid they'll

get you and make you a slave?" and "Don't
forget to stop at Dorbury when you get to running!"

Ed was usually good-natured, and met such
sallies with a grin, but a new cap and a soldier's
belt had had their effect on him, and he marched
among his deriders, very stern, dignified and
erect, as if the arduous duties of the camp were
already telling upon him. The only reply he
vouchsafed was "Nemmine, you people, nemmine. You got to git somebody else to ring yo'
ol' bell now." The crowd laughed. There came
a time when they wept at thought of that black
buffoon; the town nigger, the town drunkard,
when in the hospital and by deathbeds his touch
was as the touch of a mother; when over a
blood-swept field, he bore a woman's dearest and
nursed him back to a broken life. But no more
of that. The telling of it must be left to a time
when he who says aught of a negro's virtues will
not be cried down as an advocate drunk with
prejudice.

To the listeners outside the barracks came the
noise of grounding arms, and the talk of men relieved from duty. They were to go to their
homes until time to form in the afternoon. The
authorities were considerate. If men must go
to war, good-byes must be said, women must
weep and children cling to their fathers. The

last sad meal must be taken. The net of speculation must be thrown out to catch whatever
motes of doubt the wind of war may blow, and
the questions must fly, "Will he come back?
Shall I see him again?"

Yes, women must weep. In spite of all the
glory of war they will cling to the neck of the
departing husband, brother or son. Poor foolish
creatures; they have no eye then for the brave
array, the prancing charger and the gleaming
arms. They have no ear for the inspiring fife
and drum.

The men were soberer than they had yet been
when they filed out of the barracks. At last,
the reality of things was coming home to them.
It was all very well, this drilling on the common
in the eyes of the town, but now for the result
of their drills.

Midway among them came Tom and Walter
side by side, lieutenant and private; they had not
yet come to feel the difference in their positions.

"Well, we'll be on the way in a few hours,"
said Walter as they passed out beyond the borders of the crowd, "and I'm glad of it."

"I'm glad, too, now that we're in it, Walt, and
I'm glad to be in it myself. But it means a
whole lot, doesn't it?"

"Of course, you're leaving your family," replied Walter tentatively.

"More than that."

Both young men smiled, Walter a little bit sheepishly. He had been Tom's rival for Nannie Wood's affections, and had taken defeat at his hands.

"Oh," pursued Tom, "if the fight is going to be as short as many people think, a mere brush, in fact, we shan't be gone long—but ——"

"The people who think this is going to be a mere brush don't know the temper of the South."

"I believe you. There'll be a good many of us who won't come back."

"Oh, well, it's one time or another," and Walter smiled again as they came to the corner, and Tom turned up the street towards Nannie's house. "So long."

"So long, until this afternoon," and then the young lieutenant found himself staring straight into the eyes of Robert Van Doren. For a moment the feeling of antagonism which had shown in his conversation with Mary, surged over him, but in the next, he remembered his promise. He held out his hand.

"Hello, Bob," he said, "I guess it's hello and good-bye together."

Bob grasped his hand warmly. "Well, I reckon nobody'll be gladder to say how-dye-do to you again than I, Tom. Good luck."

"Thanks, Bob."

"Give my regards to Mary."

"I will." Tom started on. Suddenly he turned and found Van Doren watching him with a strange expression on his face. He went back and impulsively seized the other's hand. "Say, Bob, what's what?"

The blood went out of Van Doren's face. "God knows," he said in a pained voice, "that's just what I've been asking myself, and I don't know yet, Tom."

The young man paused ashamed of this show of feeling, then he said, "Well, anyway, Bob, good luck," and they went their ways.

In his heart, Tom believed that Robert Van Doren would eventually go to the Confederacy, and he resented what to him seemed flagrant disloyalty. Ohio was Van Doren's adopted home, and a tender mother she had been to him. Out of her bounty she had given him well. Now to go over to her enemies! The fight in Tom's mind as to his manner of meeting Van Doren had been brief but sharp. The result was less the outcome of generosity than the result of a subtle selfishness. It was, as all putting one's self in another's place is, the sacrifice which we make to the gods of our own desires, the concession we make to our weakness. He forgave Robert, not because Mary loved and was about to lose him, but because he, himself, loved Nannie, and for a time, at least, was about to lose her. The grasp which he gave Bob's hand meant pity for himself as well as for his sister.

There was a flash of pride on Nannie's face, though tears stood in her eyes as she saw her lover approaching. She had been expecting him and was at the gate. The soft April sunshine was playing on her gold-brown hair, and in her simple pink dimity gown she looked akin to the morning glories that blossomed about her. She opened the gate and took the young man's hand, and together they passed around the side of the house, to a rustic bench among the verbenas and sweetwilliams.

There was a simplicity and frankness about Nannie's love that was almost primitive. It was so natural, so spontaneous, so unashamed. It looked you as squarely in the face as did her coquetry. But there was no sign of coquetry now. Gone were all her whims and quips, her airs and graces. There had come into her life the transmuting element that suddenly makes a maid a woman.

For a time the two sat in silence on her flower-surrounded bench. Tom, afraid to trust his voice, and Nannie finding a certain satisfaction in merely pressing the hand she held.

Finally, he broke silence. "Well, the time is about here, Nannie."

"Yes," she replied, drawing his hand closer and caressing it, "you—you're glad, of course?"

"Glad? Well, that's a hard question. I'm glad, of course, but—but "—he struggled to grasp the elusive idea that was floating in his brain—"but there is more than one kind of being glad. I am glad, to be sure, as a citizen, and I'm sorry as a man——"

"You're sorry because——"

"You know why, little girl, I'm sorry to leave you. I'm sorry to take any chance of never being able to call you wife. It may be cowardly, but at such a time, the thought is forced irresistibly upon a man."

"It isn't cowardly, Tom, it isn't. It's manly, I know it is, because you're thinking about me. Oh, but I shall miss you when you are gone. But I'll pray for you, and I'll try to be as brave up here as you are down there. You are wrong, Tom, you are very brave, braver than the men who do not think to sorrow for the women, but go rushing into this war with a blind enthusiasm that will not let them feel. You're brave, you're brave, and I'm going to be, but I can't help it!" He caught her in his arms, and strained the weeping face to his breast.

"Darling, darling, my brave little girl, don't cry." A man is so helpless, so wordless in these times. He can do nothing but stammer and exclaim and lavish caresses.

After the first gust of weeping was over, she raised her tear-stained face, and said with a rainy smile, "I want you to understand, Tom, I'm not crying all for grief. It's just as much pride as it is sorrow. Oh, I've been spoiling your uniform." There was somewhat of a return of her old coquetry of manner, and her lover was unspeakably cheered. He had felt in that brief moment of passion as he had never felt before; how near the ocean of tears lay to the outer air and how strong was their surge against the barriers of manhood. But her change of manner gave him the courage to say the tender good-bye—the farewell too sacred to be spied upon. Ah, how his heart ached within him. How his throat swelled, and she smiled and smiled, though her eyes grew moist again. And he went on inspired by the heroism of a woman's smile, the smile she gives even when she sends her dear ones forth to face death.

He bade good-bye to Nannie's family, and went home to a sad meal and a repetition of his leave-takings.

The sister hardly succeeded as well as the sweetheart in hiding her emotions. Her heart was already heavy, and she wept, not only at the fear of death, but with the pain of love. At the very last, when he was going to take his place in the ranks, she broke down, and clung sobbing to her brother. Tom gulped, and the father, wringing his son's hands, took away her arms and comforted her as best he could. His eyes were bright and hard with the stress of the fight he was having with his feelings, but his voice was firm. Bradford Waters showed the mettle of his pasture. A New Englander, born and reared in that section of the country which has produced the most and the least emotional people, men the most conservative and the most radical; the wisest philosophers and the wildest fanatics, he did not disgrace his breeding.

It was easier for Tom, when he was once more in the ranks. Then he felt again the infectious spirit of enthusiasm which swayed his comrades. His heart beat with the drums. He heard the people cheering as they went down the street. Handkerchiefs were waving from windows and balconies, and there was a following that half walked, half trotted to keep up with the swinging stride of the soldiers. The train that was to bear them away stood puffing in the station. They crowded on. Here and there, a man dropped into his seat and buried his head in his hands, but most of the heads were out of the windows nodding good-byes. There was an air of forced gayety over it all. Young fellows with flushed cheeks laughed hard laughs, and bit their lips the moment after. It was as if no one wanted to think and yet thought would come. Children were held up to be kissed, their mothers weeping openly as is a mother's right. Fathers would start a reassuring sentence, and suddenly break off to laugh brokenly, short skeleton laughs that were sadder than tears. Then the bell gave warning and with a last rousing shout, they were off for the state capital and the chances of war.

Tom caught the last glimpse of the family and Nannie as they stood together on the platform. They were waving to him and he waved back. Nannie and Mary stood with clasped hands watching the long line of cars. On the former's face there was sorrow and pride; sorrow for her lover, pride for her soldier; but with the latter was only grief, for she could not be thoroughly loyal to her brother without feeling disloyalty to her lover. Bradford Waters walked with the crowd, but the two girls stood still, until they heard the train whistle and slacken speed as it crossed the railroad bridge, then they turned and walked back to the town. A few moments before the place had been all movement and life; now it was left to silence and tears.

CHAPTER VI

THERE was one man whom the moving glory of the departing troops filled with no elation. From a distant point, Bob Van Doren saw the blue lines swinging down the streets of Dorbury, and heard the shriek of the fifes. But there was in him no inclination to join in the shouting or to follow the admiring crowd. He was possessed neither by the joyous nor the sorrowing interest of the citizen, nor yet by the cowardly shame of the stay-at-home. While he could not go as far as his father and stay within the closed and shuttered house, yet he felt that he was not a part of the flag-flying, drum-beating throng. Many of the young fellows there were his friends who had eaten and drunk with him. They had laughed and sported together both as men and boys. But now, suddenly, it seemed that something had arisen to make them entirely different, and to put him as far apart from them and their sympathies as if they had been born at opposite poles. What was this impalpable something? he asked himself. Was it in him, in them or outside and beyond them both? Or to get at the bottom of things, did it really exist? Their training and his had been very much the same. They had gone to the same schools, read the same books and adored the same heroes. What, then, was the subtle element that had entered into life to divide them?

These were the questions he was asking himself as he heard the farewell shouts of the departing troops and the clanging of the train bell. Then he turned and with his mind full of harassing inquiries took his way home.

"Well, they're off to help rob the South of its niggers, are they?" said his father.

"They are gone," replied Robert laconically. He was not in the mood to talk.

"Humph, Southern buzzards will be the fatter for them."

"Don't, father, that's horrible. There are a good many of the fellows we both knew and liked among them."

Stephen Van Doren flashed a quick suspicious glance at his son as he remarked, "So much the worse for them."

"I wish it might have been settled some other way," pursued Robert drearily, "I'd rather have let the South secede than institute this orgie of unnatural bloodshed, brother against brother, friend against friend."

Again his father flashed that white questioning look at him. Then he rose abruptly and left the room. Robert hardly noticed the movement, so absorbed was he in his own thoughts, but sat staring blankly before him. He was momentarily aroused from his reverie by the reëntrance of his father, who laid an old miniature upon the table before him, and went out again without a word. Robert picked up the picture. It was the portrait of a beautiful young woman painted in the style of forty years before—his mother— and her name was written on a piece of yellow paper stuck in the frame, " Virginia Nelson, Fairfax Courthouse, Virginia." He gazed at the picture and read and re-read the inscription, " Fairfax Courthouse." What a quaint old-fashioned, southern sound it had. It seemed redolent of magnolias and jessamine and soft as the speech of its own citizens. But was that home, or this, the place where his youth and early manhood had been passed? Which was home, the place of memories or the place of action? What makes home; dreams or labor; the hopes of boyhood or the hard reality of later life?

To young Van Doren, the memory of his mother, who had lived only two years after coming North, had been as a guiding star and he knew that it was to recall this that his father had brought him the picture. It was apparent that he must have been strongly moved, for that little worn and faded miniature seldom left the old man's desk. His father felt deeply; so did he. His mother's eyes were pleading with him. Sentiment, said his mind; truth, said his heart.

Finally, he laid the picture face downward on the table. He told himself it must not enter into his thoughts at all. But his mind would not let it go. Eel-like, his consciousness wrapped itself about it and would not let it go. He felt guilty when the thought assailed him that perhaps the face of another woman which was graven on his heart, argued more strongly than the pictured one. "Mary, Mary," his heart said, "is my love for you blinding me to right and justice? While other men decide and do, I stand still here waiting and asking what to do." He thought of Walter Stewart and the apparent ease with which he had made a hard decision, and his anger flashed up against his own impotence; but still his inclination wavered weakly back and forth. The Union, the Confederacy; the place of his boyhood and the home of his manhood.

At last, he asked himself the question which he had so long shunned, What he believed? and he was compelled to answer that his convictions leaned to the side of those who were in arms against the general government. Then there was but one thing to do. He stood up, very pale and sad of countenance, trembling on the verge of a decision. But suddenly as out of nowhere, a voice seemed to sound into his very being, "Has love no right?" "Good God," he cried aloud, "shall I go on this way, forever wavering? Shall I go on being a coward, I who hate cowardice?" His heart was burning with pain, misery and anger and shame at himself, and yet he could not, he dared not say where he stood. The fact that he tried to fight out of recognition, and herein lay his greatest cowardice, was that he did not feel the Southern cause deeply enough to risk losing the woman he loved by its espousal; nor could he leap open-eyed into the Northern movement, for which he had no sympathy. Had he felt either as deeply as did Bradford Waters or his own father, he would not have hesitated where to take his place.

The struggle in his mind had not just begun. From the very moment that the atmosphere had become electric with the currents of opposing beliefs, he had felt himself drawn into the circuit. But, by nature, always inexpressive, he had said nothing, and left those who thought of him to the conviction that he was unmoved by passing events. But the lone nights and the grey dawns knew better. Many a time had he gone to bed after a period of earnest, self-searching, satisfied at last, and saying, " It is true, I shall take my stand," only to wake and find that everything was changed in the light of day. Many a time had morning found him in his chair where he had sat all night, trying to wrench order out of the chaos of his mind. And now, now, it was no better.

There was a step in the hall, and his father looked in on him for a moment and passed on. Robert knew that he was going through an ordeal no less terrible than his own, and he wished that it might be ended, even if it brought strife and separation between them as it had done between Walter Stewart and his father. The thought had hardly left his brain when it was occupied by another. Was he to be watched like a child who was likely to get into mischief ? This was too much, too much. He had borne with his father as long as he could. Now he would show him that he was his own master, to go his own way. Anyway, it was his concern alone. With whichever side he went, he must be shot for himself. If he stayed at home, it was he who must bear the sneers and jokes, who must live down the contumely. Whose right was it, then, to institute an annoying surveillance over him? Not even his father's. It had come to a pretty pass when a man might not think without interruption. Bah, he could not call his soul his own. It was only the sign of his nervous condition that he should fall into this state of petulant anger.

Then unaccountably, his whole mental attitude changed, and the appearance of his father's questioning face in the door, struck him only with a ludicrous aspect. He thought of himself as some coquettish but wavering maiden who bade her lover wait outside until she could answer the momentous question, yes or no, and he burst out laughing.

But his mirth was short and unnatural.

"I am either a fool or a brute," he said, "I know that father and Mary are both watching me, but they have a right to watch and they have the right to demand from me the answer in their hearts."

He paused as if a new thought had struck him. Then he rose and took his hat. "I'll do it," he exclaimed passionately, "I'll go to her and let her help me. Why haven't I thought of it before?" He passed out and called to his father as he went, "I'm going out for a while, father."

"All right," was the answer, but the words that followed solemnly were, "The boy is driven out into the street, even as the men possessed of devils spirit were driven to the rocks and the tombs. It is the evil spirit of Northern narrowness working in him."

It was with a heart somewhat lightened by the hope of relief that Robert Van Doren hastened along the street towards the Waters' home. So much had passed in the days since he had last stood at the gate that the little difference between him and the father of the woman he loved appeared as a very small thing. When two great sections of a nation are arrayed against each other, there is no time for the harboring of petty angers. Two thoughts held him. He would see Mary again. She would help him, and his honor should come to its own. These thoughts left no room in his mind for malice.

No misgiving touched him even when he stood at the door and his knock brought Mary to the door. She looked at him with a frightened face, and turned involuntarily to glance at her father who sat within.

"Is anything the matter?" she said in a low, hurried voice.

"Nothing, only I want your advice and help," said Van Doren, stepping across the threshold.

At the voice and step, Bradford Waters rose and faced the visitor, and his face began working with growing anger. "What do you mean by invading my house, again, Robert Van Doren?"

"I came to see Mary."

Waters took his daughter by the hand as if he would put himself between the girl and her lover. "Mary can have no dealings with you or your kind. We do not want you here. I have told you that before. Your way and ours lie apart."

"They have not always lain apart and need not now." Van Doren's surprise was stronger than his resentment as he looked into the old man's passionate face. Could a few days work such a change in a man?

"They must and shall lie apart," Waters took him up hotly. "What you have been to this family, you cannot be again."

"What have I done to forfeit your respect?"

"It isn't what you've done, but what you are."

"How do you know what I am?"

"That's it. At least, your father has the courage to come out and say what he is. You haven't. At least, he is a man ——"

"Father, father," cried Mary, "don't say any more!"

"I'm sorry to see a daughter of mine," said Waters, turning upon her, "pleading for one of those whom her brother has gone South to kill." The girl put her hands up quickly as if she would check the words upon her father's lips. Van Doren had turned very white. He stood as one stunned. All his hopes of help had been suddenly checked, and instead of sympathy, he had received hard words. But a smile curved his lips.

"Have I not said enough, Robert Van Doren?"

"Yes," was the reply, still with a quiet smile, "you have said enough," and he turned towards the door.

Mary sprang away from her father. "Robert, Robert, don't go," she cried, "he doesn't mean it. This great trouble has made him mad." Bradford Waters started to speak but stopped as the young man put off the girl's detaining hand. "I must go, Mary," he said, "your father is right. We have come to the parting of the ways. I have not had the courage to say where I stood, but I have it now. I came for help to decide a momentous question. I have got it. Good-bye, Mary, good-bye—Mr. Waters, the Confederacy may thank you for another recruit."

He opened the door and passed out, the old man's voice ringing after him, "Better an open rebel than a copperhead." A hard look came into the girl's eyes.

"You needn't worry," said her father, "it's good riddance." She made no reply.

In spite of all that passed, Robert Van Doren went home in a lighter frame of mind.

"I'm going to leave to-morrow," he said to his father.

"You have made your choice?"

"The South needs me," returned the young man evasively. His father came to him and kissed him on both cheeks. Then he took the miniature from the table and placed it on his breast.

"I knew that your mother would not plead with you in vain," he said, and Robert smiled bitterly.

CHAPTER VII

DIVIDED HOUSES

THERE is a tragic quietness about a town whose best and bravest have gone to a doubtful battlefield. The whole place seems hushed and on tiptoe as if listening for some sound from the field. The cry of a cricket shivers the silenee into splinters of sound, and each one pierces the ear with a sharpness which is almost pain. It was under such a pall of stillness that Dorbury lay immediately after the departure of the troops. It was not altogether the torpor that succeeds an upheaval. Part of it was the breathless silence of expectancy, as when from a height some one hurls a boulder into space and waits to hear it fall. Of course, it would be some time before they could expect to hear from the new soldiers, and yet, Dorbury listened, expectant hand to ear.

The spring sunshine, not yet strong nor violent enough to destroy its own sweetness, fell with a golden caress on the quiet streets. To some, who went to and fro, bowed with anxiety, it seemed strange that in such a time, nature should go on performing her processes as she had always done. Their hearts seemed to stand still, but time went on, the flowers bloomed, the grasses sprung and the restless river sang to the silent town.

The tension of suspense had told greatly upon Bradford Waters' character. From being a gentle father, he had grown to be short, almost harsh to Mary. His love and fear for his soldier son had made him blind to the pain his daughter suffered.

He was so far gone in the earnestness of his views that he could see nothing but a perverse disloyalty in his daughter's feeling towards Robert Van Doren. His friendship for the young fellow had changed with the changing of the times, and he could not understand that a woman's love may be stronger than her politics; her heart truer to its affections than her head to its principles.

It can hardly be said of Mary that she felt more than she thought, but her emotions were stronger than her convictions. It was the worse for her state of mind that for two widely different reasons, the taking of her brother and the estrangement from her lover, she was placed in a resentful position against the cause that she naturally would have espoused.

Still, at first, she kept a certain appearance of

loyalty, and when some of the girls with impet-
uous enthusiasm, started a sewing circle for the
soldiers, she joined with them, and began to ply
her needle in the interest of the Union troops.
But among these friends of undivided interests,
it was not always pleasant for Mary. All about
her, she heard sentiments that did not comport
with the feelings of one who had loved ones on
both sides of the great question. Over the lint
and flannels that passed through the sewers'
hands, were made several hot and thoughtless
speeches that seared the very soul of one poor
girl. They were not intentional. Most of them,
had they known that one among them suffered
from their unthinking remarks, would have held
their tongues. Others, not more than one or
two, be it said, knew that every sneer they cast
at the army of the South, every hard wish they
expressed, tore like an arrow through the tender
heart of the pale sad girl in the corner who bent
so silently over her work.

"I do wish," said little Martha Blake one day,
"that the whole Southern army was drowned in
the depths of the sea. They are so troublesome."

"What would their sisters do?" asked Mary
quietly.

"Oh, really, they seem such monsters to me
that I never thought of their having sisters."

Mary smiled. "And yet they have," she said,

"some of them, perhaps, making just as foolish a wish about our brothers as you have made about them."

"I know it's foolish," Martha pursued, "but it has never seemed to me that those people down there who have done so much to tempt the Northern government are quite the same as we are."

Unconsciously, Mary took the defensive and stepped over into the point of view of the man whom in her heart she was defending.

"But why," she exclaimed, "do you say the Northern government? The very mention of the word denies the principle for which we claim we are fighting—that there is no North, no South, but one country inseparable into sections."

"I had never thought of that," said Martha.

"I don't think any of us have thought of it," put in Anice Crowder, "except those who have very dear friends among the traitors."

Mary turned deadly pale for she knew that Bob Van Doren's decision had just become generally known. She turned a pair of flashing eyes on Anice as she replied,

"No man is a traitor who fights for what he believes to be right."

"Any man is a traitor who lives under one flag and leaves it to fight under another."

"A man is accountable only to his conscience and his God."

"Yes, when he has proved traitor to every other tie, only then."

The words cut Mary like a knife. She rose, work in hand and stood quivering with passion as she looked down on her insulter.

"Then the woman who cares for such a man, who dares stand up for him is a traitor too?" she cried as she flung her work to the floor.

"Yes," said Anice acidly.

Mary started towards the door, but a chorus of girls' voices checked her.

"Don't go, Mary," they cried, "we know, we don't blame you." But the girl's heart was overburdened, and bursting into tears, she fled from the room. She heard the hubbub of voices as she went hastily out of the house, and even in that moment of grief she was glad that some of the girls there would be quick to defend her. She knew who must have been foremost in this defence when she heard a light step behind her and felt Nannie Woods' arm about her waist.

"Don't cry, Mary," said Nannie soothingly. "No one minds Anice Crowder or anything she says. Anyway, I gave her a good piece of my mind before I left there, and so did some of the rest of the girls. I just told her right to her face that she'd have more feeling for people if she had a lover on either side."

Mary was forced to smile a little at her friend's impetuosity. But from her heart she thanked the girl, and drew her arm tighter about her waist.

"I suppose Anice thinks that I can send my love where I will, and that I am to blame if it does not go in the right, or what she thinks, the right direction."

"She's a cat," was the emphatic rejoinder, "and I for one, will never go to their old sewing-circle. We'll sew together, just you and I, Mary, and while I'm making things for Tom, there's no reason why you shouldn't make a keepsake for Bob to take with him."

Mary gasped.

"Oh, that's all right, I know if I lived down South and it was Tom, I'd —— "

"Hush, Nannie," said Mary hurriedly, "you mustn't say those things."

"I will say them and I don't care."

They reached the Waters' gate and the girls parted. There, for Nannie, the incident closed, but it was destined to cause Mary Waters even more suffering.

Women's sewing circles are not usually noted for their reticence, and the institution at Dorbury was no exception. Within an hour after it happened, the whole affair was out to the town, and the story in a highly embellished form reached Bradford Waters' ears.

He went home in a white passion. Mary had got supper and was sitting idly by the window when her father burst into the room. She looked up and saw on the instant that he had heard.

"What is this I hear of you at the sewing-circle?"

"I suppose you have heard the truth or part of it."

"So it has come to the pass where my daughter must defend a former copperhead and now an avowed rebel!"

"The man whom I defended, if defence it could be called, was to me neither copperhead nor rebel. He was my lover. I have nothing to do with his politics. The war has nothing to do with my love."

She was calmer than usual, and her very quietness exasperated her father the more.

"I'll have no more of it," he cried passionately, "I'll have no more of it. Love or no love, a house divided against itself cannot stand. My house must be with me. And if my daughter feels called upon to go over to the enemy's side, she must go over to the enemy's house. My house shall not shelter her."

"Father —— "

"Enough, I have said my say. You must abide by it. I'll have no more such stories as I have heard to-day poured into my ears. Either give up that renegade or take your love for him to another roof."

He flung himself petulantly into a chair and fell to his supper. Mary did not answer him, only a look of hard defiance came into her gentle eyes. It might have struck Bradford Waters had he seen it, but he did not look at her again.

A little kindness might have done much to soften the rigor of Mary's feelings, and so changed the course of events; for she was easily swayed through her affections. She would not have given up Van Doren, his hold upon her was too strong. But she would have repressed herself even to the hiding of her feelings, had she not been driven into the open revolt to which her father's harsh treatment goaded her. Now the determination to be true to her lover at all hazards came upon her so strongly that her attitude really became one of aggression.

It was now that the remembrance of Nannie's thoughtless words came to her, and she asked herself, "Why not?" Why should she not make and give Van Doren a keepsake to take into the ranks with him? She had suffered sorrow for his sake; in effect, she had been forcibly, almost involuntarily, cast on his side. She had to withstand contempt and reviling. Would this one show of affection be so much more?

That evening, Mary was very busy sewing, and so part of the next day, until the time when her father came home. Then she hastened to leave her stitching to go about her supper, for in the absorption of her new idea, she had neglected it.

Bradford Waters looked at the work which had stood between him and his meals with an ill-concealed exasperation. Why couldn't women sew at the proper time and leave off properly? Maybe, though, it was something for her brother Tom. If that were so, he did not care. He would go without his meals any time, that Tom might have a single comfort. Bless the brave boy. His face softened, and he looked with filling eyes as his mind dwelt on tender memories of the soldier son. Suddenly the bit of embroidery there on the shelf seemed to take on a new interest for him.

Mary was crossing the floor with a plate in her hand, when he rose and going to the shelf, picked up the work. She made an involuntary motion as if to stop him and take it away, then she paused rigid.

He stood smiling down on the sewing. "Something for Tom," he began, and then the smile froze and the words died on his lips as he turned it over. It was only a little maroon housewife such as any soldier might need in the emergencies of camp life, but on its front were embroidered the letters, " R. V. D."

He stood gazing at them for a moment as if they were cabalistic, and the mystery was just filtering through his mind. Then, with trembling hands, he threw it across the room.

"My God," he cried, " and I thought it was for her brother! And it is for the comfort of the enemy!"

"It is only a keepsake," said Mary faintly. She was frightened and weakened by his agitation.

He looked at her as if he saw her but dimly, then he said in a hard voice, " This is the end of all. Pick it up," pointing to the housewife. " Now go. Take the visible evidence of your treason and go, and may God and your poor brother forgive you. I never shall."

At another time, Mary might have pleaded with him, but she was dazed, and before she had recovered her presence of mind, her father had left the house. Then she too, as if still in a dream, picked up the offending gift and went out.

She could not understand her father. She did not know what the gift to the enemy meant to him. How he felt as if a serpent had stung him from his own hearth.

She went mechanically, at first, scarce knowing which way she tended. Then thought came to her, and with the keepsake still in her hand, she turned dry-eyed towards Nannie Woods' house.

"It was such a little thing," she murmured as she went into the house, and then suddenly, unconsciousness came to her.

CHAPTER VIII

AS A MAN THINKETH IN HIS HEART

WHEN Mary recovered consciousness, it was to find herself lying in Nannie's own bed and her friend beside her. For a moment, she did not remember what had happened, and then the full flood tide of recollection swept over her mind. She buried her head on Nannie's bosom and sobbed out her story.

"Never mind," said Nannie, "never mind, you're going to come here and stay with me, that's what you are going to do. No hardhearted fathers are going to bother you, that's what they're not."

Say what you will, there is always something of the child left in every woman, and though the soft-hearted girl talked and cooed to Mary as she would have done to a restless child, the heart broken woman was soothed by it.

" Don't you think father ought to understand, Nannie? It isn't because Robert is a copperhead or a rebel, whichever he is, that I love him, but in spite of it."

"Mary," said Nannie, and her voice was meditative and her face dreamy, "don't you know there never was a man yet who knew how or why a woman loved?" A new wisdom, a half playful wisdom though it was, seemed to have come to the girl. Some women never grow clear-sighted until their eyes are opened to the grey form of an oncoming sorrow. Nannie was of this class. "But," she went on laughing, "it's all the fault of Father Adam. Men are so much the sons of their fathers, and it all comes of giving him the first woman while he was asleep and not letting him know when nor how."

"And yet men do love," said Mary seriously.

"Oh, of course they love, but —" the girls' eyes met and both of them blushed. "It won't last long anyhow, Mary, so what's the use of being sad? Let's talk about them." Nannie cuddled down close to the bed.

"About whom?" was the deceitful question.

"Oh, you minx, you know whom. What's the use of asking? I wonder where Tom is to-night?"

"It's hard telling, they've been delaying them so much along the road."

"I don't think it's right at all. They rushed them off toward Washington, and I think they ought to be allowed to get there. How's a man

going to distinguish himself if he can't get any-
where within sight of the enemy?"

"I haven't your spirit, Nannie, I wish I had.
I forget all about distinction. I only wonder
how it's all going to turn out, and if those I love
are coming back to me."

"Oh, Mary, don't be like that. Of course,
they're coming back, Tom and Rob and all of
them, and we're going to be happy again, and
there won't be any such names called as copperhead and rebel and abolitionist. Let me show
you what I've made for Tom. I'd have given it
to him before he went away, but it was all so
sudden. Oh, my!" and for an instant the girl
dropped her chin upon her hands and sat staring
into Mary's eyes without seeing her. Then she
sprang up and darted away. In a few minutes
she returned bearing with her some mysterious
piece of feminine handiwork over which the two
fell into the sweet confidences so dear to their
age and sex.

Nannie, light and frivolous as she seemed, had
a deep purpose in her mind. She saw clearly
that the serious, not to say, morbid cast, of
Mary's character, would drive her to lay too
much importance upon her father's act and so
perhaps, let it prove more injurious to her than
was necessary. Without Mary's depth, she saw
more clearly than Bradford Waters' daughter

that a little space of madness was at hand, and every deed had to be judged not by its face alone, but by its face as affected by the surrounding atmosphere, just as the human countenance shows ghastly in one light and ruddy in another, without really changing. So she strove to draw her companion's thought away from her sorrows and to avert the dangers she anticipated. She succeeded only in part. After awhile, Mary fell into a light sleep, but on the morrow she awoke with a raging fever. The strain on her nerves had been too great and she had succumbed to it.

At the first intimation of danger to his daughter, Nannie had bid her father hasten to notify Bradford Waters.

"It's no use," said Nathan Woods, "Waters is more set in his views than any man I ever saw. If he believes that he had reason to send her out of his house, not even death itself could take her back there unless those reasons were destroyed. I know Bradford Waters, and he's a hard man."

But the young woman insisted, and, as usual, had her way. Her father went to Waters. There was not much tact or finesse about his approach. He found his neighbor sitting down to a lonely breakfast, and depositing his hat on the floor, after an embarrassed silence, he began.

"Kind of lonesome, eh?"

"These are no times for men to be lonesome.

The Lord makes every loyal man a host in himself."

"That's good, and yet it isn't the kind of host that crowds on each other's toes and cracks jokes to keep the time a-going."

"You're irreverent, Nathan, and besides, this is no time to be cracking jokes. The hour has come when the cracking of rifles is the only thing."

"I didn't mean to be irreverent, and I'm afraid you don't understand. I've come for your own good, Waters. The little girl sent me. Don't you think you're doing wrong?"

"No, as the god of battles is my judge, no!" Waters' eyes were blazing, and he had forgotten his breakfast.

"Your daughter is at my house, and she is sick, very sick."

"I have no daughter."

"God gave you one."

"He also said that a house divided against itself cannot stand."

"What of that?"

"My house is my son Tom and myself."

"What of your daughter, Mary?"

Waters turned upon him his sad bright eyes, sad in spite of their hardness.

"If thy right hand offend thee, cut it off," he said, with a slashing gesture.

"That's not right," said Nathan Woods. "It's not right, I say, to be using the Scripture to stand between you and your daughter."

"I have no daughter. The daughter I had has gone out after other gods than mine."

The old New England fanaticism, the Puritanical intolerance, was strong in the man.

"My God," exclaimed his opposer, "quit mutilating the Bible to bolster up your own pride. Mary's sick, she's sick enough to die, maybe."

"If she die away from home, it is God's will, perhaps his punishment," said Waters solemnly.

"Is it Jepthah and his daughter?"

"No, it is David and Absalom."

Nathan Woods got up; he looked long and hard at his old friend. Then, taking his hat from the floor, he started for the door. There he paused.

"And the war has done this," he said slowly. "Well, Bradford, I say damn the war."

The lonely father sat down again to his breakfast, but the food disgusted him.

Mary sick and away from home. What would Tom say? What would Tom have done? But then the memory of the whole wrong she had done him and her brother came back upon the old man, and he shut his teeth hard. It was a crime. It was treason. Let her go her way and die among the people who were

willing to condone her faults. He could not.
It was not flesh and blood, but soul and spirit
that counted now. It was not that the South
had touched his body, and that Mary had
sided with them. It was that a rebellious section had touched not his soul, but the soul of his
country, and his daughter had bade them Godspeed. This was the unforgivable thing. This
was the thing that put the girl outside the
pale of parental pardon. So thinking, he rose
from the table and went out of the disordered
house.

Dorbury was a town of just the size where
any one's business is every one's else. So it was
an impossibility that the breach between Mary and
her father should long remain a secret. A half-
dozen neighbors knew the story an hour after
the doctor had left Nathan Woods' door, and had
told it in varying degrees of incorrectness.

One gossip said that Waters' daughter had
sought to elope with Robert Van Doren, had even
got as far as the railway station, when her father
had found her and brought her back. She was
now imprisoned at the Woods', with Nannie to
watch her.

Another knew on good authority that Mary had
denounced the Union, declared her intention of
doing all she could to aid the Confederacy, and had
then fled from home to escape from her father's

just wrath. Anice Crowder's story of the affair in the sewing-circle gave color to this view of the case.

Still, another, however, told how Robert Van Doren's sweetheart, mad for love of him, and crazed at the choice he had made, went wandering about the streets until friendly hands took her to Nannie's door. One man had helped to take her there.

So the rumors flew from lip to lip like shuttle-cocks and the story grew with the telling of it.

It would have been strange then, if it had not reached the ears of the Van Dorens. Indeed, it came to them on the first morning. Stephen Van Doren chuckled.

"You're making a great stir for one poor copperhead," he said to his son. "You've made the wolf's stir in the Waters' sheepfold. If you'll only cause the Yankees as much trouble when you have a musket in your hand, I shall have reason to be proud of my son."

Robert turned angrily upon his father.

"I wish you wouldn't talk that way about the matter, father. I don't like all this talk about Mary, and I wish I could stop it. If the girl is suffering on account of loyalty to me, God bless her. It's as little as my father could do to speak respectfully of her sacrifice."

"You do not understand me, Robert, I do not

laugh at the girl. It is at her father and his folly that I laugh."

"My love for his daughter makes the father sacred to me."

"It must be a very strong love that makes Bradford Waters sacred."

"My love for Mary is deeper and stronger than any political prejudice that you or I might have."

"Very well, Bob, very well, go your own way. My business is not with your love, but with your politics; if the latter be all right I shall not worry about the former."

Robert Van Doren spent little time after hearing of Mary's illness, but betook himself immediately to her door. Nannie met him and drew him inside.

"I am so sorry," she began before he could tell his errand, "but you cannot see her. She is very sick and excitable. Oh, Robert, isn't it awful, this war and all that it is bringing to us?"

"I wish it were over. Is Mary delirious?"

"At times, and when she isn't, we could almost wish she were; she is so piteous."

"Her father has been hard upon her."

"Yes, that's because he's delirious too. Every one is mad, you and I and all of us. When shall we come to our senses?"

"God knows. Will you give Mary this?" He

drew off his glove and laid it in Nannie's hand. "Tell her it is forbidden me to say good-bye to her, but I leave this as a pledge, and when I may, I shall come back and redeem it."

There were tears on Nannie's face as he turned toward the door. With an impulsive movement, she sprang forward and laid her hand on his arm. "You may kiss me," she said, "and I will bear it to her, and place it on her lips as you would have done."

Robert paused, and bent over her lips as he might have done over Mary's, and then with a wave of his hand, he was gone and the door behind him closed. Nannie turned and went to Mary's room where she laid the glove on the pillow beside the pale face of the unconscious girl. Her brow was fevered and her hair dishevelled, and every now and then incoherent words forced themselves between her parched lips.

"I might have let him see her for a minute, but it was better not to. He would only have gone away with the misery of it in his heart." Then Nannie stooped and kissed her friend's lips. "There, Mary," she said, "it's from him. Oh, my dear, dear girl, if your father could see you now, I believe even his heart would melt towards you."

But Bradford Waters was not to see her then.

With bowed head and slow steps, eaten by grief, anger and anxiety, he made his way towards the tobacco warehouse where he spent a large part of the day among his employees. The place had never seemed quite the same to him since the first day Tom had been absent from his desk. He was thinking of him now as he went cheerlessly along. What a head for business the boy had. How much more of a success he would be than ever his father had been. How the men loved him already. It was no wonder that Mary —but Mary —— He checked his thoughts and set his teeth hard. There was no Mary, no sister any more. She had broken the tie that bound her to Tom and him. He said this to himself because he did not know how women wrench and tear their hearts to keep from breaking ties that war with each other.

He was absorbed in such thoughts when some one hailed him from a doorway.

"What news?" said a gentleman stepping out and joining him in his walk.

"No news, except of delay," said Waters in a dissatisfied tone.

"Where is the gallant First now?"

They were already the "Gallant First" although they had not yet got within powder-smelling distance of the enemy.

"The gallant First is being delayed and played

with somewhere between Columbus and Washington."

"Why should that be?"

"It all comes of electing a gentleman governor."

"Why now, Waters," said Davies, smilingly. "There is surely no objection to a governor's being a gentleman?"

"There's some objection to his being nothing else."

"You remind me a good deal of the Methodists and the devil; whatever bad happens, they are never at a loss to know where to put the blame. I sometimes think that maybe the devil is painted a little black, and likewise, maybe, Dennison isn't to blame for everything that goes wrong in the handling of this situation."

Waters took this sally with none too good a grace. Davies was suspected of being lukewarm in the Union cause, and some had even accused him of positive Southern sympathies. He was a wealthy, polished, easy-going man, and his defence of Governor Dennison, whose acts every one felt free to blame at that time, was more because he sympathized with that gentleman's aristocratic tastes and manners than because he wished delay to the progress of the Union's forces.

"So you think it's Dennison who's delaying the

troops, do you ? " he went on in a light, bantering tone.

" I think nothing about it, I only know that
our boys went rushing away to the state capital,
and under the impression that Washington was
menaced, were sent flying east half equipped and
totally unprepared for the conflict, and I do know
that despite their haste, they have not reached
their destination yet."

" For which, of course, the devil is to blame ? "

" Whoever is to blame, this is no time for a
banqueting, bowing, speech-making governor.
We need a man of action in the chair now, if we
ever did. Look how things are going at Columbus. Troops flocking there, no provision made
for them. Half of them not knowing whether
they are to be accepted or not and the dandy
who calls himself the chief executive sits there
and writes letters. My God, what have we
come to ! "

" Have you ever thought that even a governor
needs time to adjust himself to a great crisis ?
Is it not true that the authorities of the general
government insisted on the regiment in which
your son's company is placed going directly to
Washington ? "

" Then why are they not there instead of dally-
ing about, heaven knows where, while a lot of
other fellows are being quartered at the Colum-

bus hotels at extortionate prices which the tax-payers must pay ? "

" Are you measuring your patriotism by dol-lars and cents ? "

" I'm measuring my patriotism by the greatest gift that any one could make to his country, his only son. Have you an equal measure ? "

" No, but I have some confidence in my state and my country's officers, and that is worth some-thing in a time like this. Now don't get hot in the collar, Waters, but you wait awhile and give Dennison and the government time."

" Yes, wait, wait, that's been the cry right along. Wait until every road this side the capi-tal of the country is blocked and from Maryland and Virginia the rebels march victorious into Washington. Don't talk to me of waiting, Davies, we have waited too long already, that's what's the matter."

Davies laughed lightly as he turned down the street which led to his own office.

Bradford Waters' intemperance was a great index of the spirit of the time as it was mani-fested in Ohio. Governor Dennison was too slow for the radicals ; too swift for the conservatives, and incompetent in the opinion of both. Noth-ing could happen, except what was good, nothing could go wrong but that he was blamed for it. All the men who volunteered could not be accepted and Dennison was to blame. The soldiers were delayed enroute and Dennison was to blame. Rations were scarce and prices high and Dennison was to blame, and so all the odium that attaches to a great war which strikes a people unprepared for it, fell upon the head of the hapless executive.

CHAPTER IX

IN the days which followed the separation between Mary and himself, Bradford Waters was indeed a lonely man. He was harassed not only by the breach with the child he loved and the public comments upon it, but torn with anxiety for Tom. He spent his days and nights in brooding that made him harder and bitterer as time went on. His fanatical dislike for Stephen Van Doren grew because this man and his family seemed to him the author of all his woes. He was not only just a copperhead, now, with a son in the Confederate army, he stood as the personification of the whole body of rebellion that had taken Waters' son and daughter and broken up his home. He could have no pride in his soldier boy without cursing Van Doren for being one of those who had driven him into danger. He could not grieve for the loss of Mary without sending his imprecations flying in the same direction. Always to his distorted vision, his old-

time enemy appeared as some relentless monster
grinning in terrible glee at his distress.

Despite his moroseness, however, there was a
wistful, almost plaintive attitude in Waters' conduct towards his acquaintances. He hovered between moods of grief, anxiety and pride. But
always, at the last, the innate hardness of his nature triumphed. There were times when his
heart cried out for Mary, for some one of his
blood to share his grief with him. But he
closed his lips and uttered no word to bring her
back to him. Always a simple-living man, accustomed to no service save that of his own family, he was compelled to employ a servant, and
this galled him, not out of penuriousness, but because he could not bear an alien in his home.
He felt her eyes upon him at moments when it
seemed that the struggle in his heart must be
written large upon his face, and it filled him
with dumb, helpless anger.

A change, too, was taking place in Van Doren.
Now that he had a son in the field, he had a new
feeling for his friend and enemy. Besides being
a partisan, he was a father and the paternal instinct prompted him to change his actions towards Waters. Had the two old men let themselves, they would have poured out their fears,
hopes and anxieties to each other, and found relief and sympathy. Both affectionate fathers,

similarly bereft of sons and similarly alone, they might have been a comfort to each other, but that their passions forbade their fraternizing. Often they met upon the streets and Van Doren would look at Waters with a question in his eyes. It would have been such a natural thing to say, "Any news of Tom?" and to be asked in the same tone, "What of Bob?" But Waters always scowled fiercely although he kept his head averted. So each, smothering down the yearning in his heart for companionship and sympathy passed on his way with a curb bit on his emotions.

It was about this time that dispatches from the front gave warning that a sharp, though brief encounter had taken place between the rebels and a detachment of troops under General Schenck. The news ran like wildfire through Dorbury, for it was at first rumored and then assured that the First, to which the home company belonged, had been engaged and had lost several men. Every home out of which a husband, son or father had gone, waited with breathless expectancy, longing, yet dreading to hear more definite tidings from the field. The people about every fireside clustered closer together with blanched faces, wondering if their circle had been touched. This was war indeed, and with the first fear for their loved ones, came the first realization of what it really meant.

At first, Bradford Waters tried hard to restrain himself. He gripped his hands hard and paced up and down the room. But finally, he could stand it no longer. The house had grown close and unbearable. Its walls seemed to be narrowing in upon him like the sides of a torture chamber. He hurried out into the street and into the telegraph office. There was no further news. Then to the office of the one remaining paper. Their bulletin furnished nothing further. For two hours he paced back and forth between these two places, feverish and disturbed. Van Doren saw him pass back and forth on his anxious tramp, and his own heart interpreted the other's feelings. Once, the impulse came to him to speak to Waters, and he rose from the window where he had been sitting, and went to the door, but the crazed man turned upon him such a grey, haggard face and withal so fierce and unfriendly, that he retreated from his good intentions, and let him pass on unchallenged.

The next day the news was better. The papers said that the casualties had been almost nothing.

Waters' hopes rose, and he showed a more cheerful face to those who saw him. Maybe Tom was safe, after all, maybe he had been gallant in action, and would be promoted. His heart throbbed with joy and pride as if what he wished were already a fact. It is a strange thing about home people in war time that after the first pang of anxiety is over, the very next thought is one of ambition. They seem all to see but two contingencies for their loved ones, death or promotion. It happened that there was not a single engagement of the war, however small or insignificant, but it gave some home circle a thrill of hope that one who was dear to them might have moved up a notch in the notice and respect of his country. It was not narrowness nor was it the lust for personal advancement. It was rather the desire of those who give of their best to serve a beloved cause to have them serve it in the highest and most responsible position possible.

Meanwhile, to Mary slowly recovering her strength and balance, had come much of the anxiety which racked her father. With the inconsistent faith of a woman, she said that God could not have let her brother fall in this first fight, and she prayed that he might be restored to them safe. And even before the breath of her declaration and prayer had cooled on her lips, she wept as she pictured him dead on the roadside.

Later, it is true, these people's hearts came to be so schooled in the terrible lessons of civil war that they let such light skirmishes as this one at

Vienna give them little uneasiness. But then, they did not know.

Bradford Waters' great joy came to him two days after the papers had lightened his care. There was a list of the wounded and killed, and Tom's name was not among them. Then came his letter.

"Dear father," it ran, "I suppose you've been in horrible suspense about me, and a good deal of it is my fault. But when a fellow is learning entirely new things, among them how to write without any sort of writing materials under the sun, it isn't easy, is it? Then, too, I've been trying to learn to be a soldier. It's awfully different, this being a militiaman and a soldier. In the first place, a militiaman may curse his governor. A soldier must not. It's been hard refraining, but I haven't cursed Dennison as I wanted to. Some of the fellows say he's all right, but we've been delayed on the way here by first one thing and then another until the patience of all of us is worn out. If it isn't Governor Dennison's fault, whose is it? I wish you'd find out. We fellows don't know, and can't find out anything. The generals just take us wherever they please and never consult us about anything. But I'm used to that now.

"Of course, you've heard about the trouble at Vienna, and I was afraid you'd be considerably worried. It wasn't anything much. Only it was different from a muster day. Some rebels fired on our train unexpectedly, but we tumbled out helter-skelter and fired back at them, and so they let us alone. It didn't seem quite fair to jump on a fellow when he wasn't looking, but I guess this is war.

"There isn't a thing to do about Washington these days. It's as safe as a meeting-house. There are some New York troops here that I have got acquainted with, but we don't any of us do anything but look pretty. Some of the fellows are already looking forward to the mustering out day. But mustered out or not, I'm going to hang around here, for there's no telling when things are going wrong, and for my part, I expect more trouble. A set of fellows who will fire on their own flag as they did at Sumter are perfectly capable of lying low until they quiet our suspicions and then raising the very dickens.

"Give Mary my love, and tell her she ought to see Washington and all the pretty girls here that cheer us as we go along the streets. (Tell her to read this part of the letter to Nannie. I'm going to write her anyway in a day or two, but now it's all go, go, go, learn, learn, learn.) Take care of yourself, father, or rather let Mary take care of you, for you would never think of it. I'll write you again when I get a chance.

"Your son,
"TOM."

Bradford Waters could have wept for joy over his son's letter, but that he felt weeping to be unworthy of a soldier's father. The battle of Vienna had been fought and his son had come out safe. He thought of it as a Thermopylæ when it was only a petty skirmish. A few rebels fired at a few Unionists, who lined themselves up against their cars and returned the fire. This was all, but he preferred to think of his son as one of a band of heroes who at great odds had repelled the assailants of their country's flag, and held the day against armed treason.

One thing grieved him greatly, the reference to Mary. He could not tell her nor talk it over with her. She take care of him! What would her brother think if he knew how they were living, and he was going to write to Nannie? Would she not tell him all, and what encouragement would this be to the boy in the field when he knew how matters were going at home? Bradford Waters' hand trembled and the letter burned in his fingers.

Notwithstanding his perplexity, when Waters appeared on the streets that day, Stephen Van Doren seeing him, did not need to inquire to know that the Unionist had received a welcome letter from his son, and secretly, he rejoiced at it. Knowing as he did, that the time would come when anxiety for his own boy would tear at his heart, he could not begrudge the other man his joy. He was pleased, too, because as he passed Waters and looked into his beaming face, there seemed almost an inclination on his part to stop and speak.

Indeed, the old Unionist did want to stop and say, "Stephen, I've heard from Tom, and he's all right." He did not, and the repression only made him long the more for Mary. He wanted her to see his letter, to know that her brother was being cheered by the women of Washington, and to feel what he felt. But would she feel so? Had not her heart already gone too strongly to the other side? The question came again to him, and he hardened again in face of it.

He would not tell her nor send the letter to her. She was a traitor. But he would let her know that he had received it. So that afternoon, he talked much of his letter in the places where men congregate, and told what Tom had said, and Mary heard of it from others and burned with eagerness.

That night, as soon as darkness had fallen, eluding Nannie's vigilance, she crept out of the house. She made her way to her own home, and back and forth before the door, she walked and kept vigil. Maybe her father would see her and come out and tell her more of Tom. Maybe he would understand and forgive her and she could go back to him again. But she wished in vain, and after a time, her heart unsatisfied, she went back to Nannie's, and silently let herself in.

It was after midnight, when Waters crept out of his house, and with feverish steps made his way to the Woods' door. For a long time he walked up and down before the place even as Mary had done, and then, as if struck with a sudden determination, he opened the gate and going to the door, slipped the letter under it. Then he turned away home, feeling lighter and better because he had shared his joy with his daughter.

CHAPTER X

SORROW MAY LAST FOR A NIGHT

IT was of a piece with the proverbial blindness of man that Nathan Woods should have stepped over the letter as he went out in the morning without taking note of it, just as it was natural to the keen sight of woman that Nannie should see it the first thing as she came down in the morning. She ran swiftly towards it and cast her eye over the address. At first she gasped, then she awoke the echoes with a joyous shriek and went flying up to Mary's room. Mary sat up in bed in dumb amazement which was only increased when the enthusiastic girl threw her arms about her and began sobbing and laughing alternately.

"Oh, Mary," she cried, "it's come, it's come, and he's all right."

"What is it, Nannie? What's come, and who's all right?"

"Your father's been here, oh!"

"My father? When? What did he say?"

"Nothing, oh, I didn't see him, he didn't say anything."

"I don't understand you, Nannie. You say my father didn't say anything at all?"

"Why, how could he? He came at night, and he didn't say anything because he couldn't, you know. We were all asleep, but he left this." She broke off her violent demonstrations long enough to thrust the letter into Mary's hand, then she immediately resumed them with such a degree of fervor that her friend found it impossible to get a glimpse of the missive she held in her hand. Gently, at last, she put her hand aside, and then trembling with anticipation, glanced at the letter. Her face fell.

"But this is not addressed to me," she said.

"Oh, you great goose, don't you see, that it's to your father and from Tom and that he wanted you to know? Else why should he have slipped it under the door?"

"Do you think he did it, really?"

"Of course, he did, who else? He couldn't lose it crawling into our hallway, and that's the only other way it could have got there."

"I wonder if I ought to read it?" mused Mary fingering the envelope eagerly, but nervously.

"Mary Waters!" exclaimed Nannie, "if you don't read that letter this instant, I'll take it from you and read it myself."

"That's right, do, Nannie, you're braver than I am," and Mary proffered the letter. But Nannie sprang back with sudden timidity.

"No, I won't," she said. "It's for you, but if it were my brother's letter, I'd have read it long before now."

"Well, I'll read it, if you'll stay and hear it," and she took the penciled sheets out and began the perusal of the words which had brought so much joy to her father's heart. As she read, the color came back to her faded cheeks and the light to her eyes. Her bosom heaved with pleasure and pride. Nannie was no less delighted. As the reading went on, she continued to give Mary little encouraging hugs, and she was radiant.

Then came the passage about the girls.

"Humph," said Nannie, "is that all a soldier has to write about? I should think he'd be thinking more about the safety of his country than about the girls he sees."

"Oh, you know he's only funning, Nannie, and then he says Washington's as safe as a meeting-house."

"I don't believe it. I believe the rebels are waiting to swoop down on the city at any time and capture all our state papers, and archives and things, wherever they keep them, while our soldiers go around looking pretty for the girls to cheer. Humph!"

Mary kissed her and laughed, and the rest of the reading proceeded without demonstrations from Tom's sweetheart. At its close, she made no comment whatever, but sat upon the bed swinging her feet with pronounced indifference.

"Aren't you glad to hear from him?" said Mary merrily, "and to find him in such good spirits? Dear old Tom. And wasn't it good of father to bring his letter to me? Didn't I tell you, Nannie, that my father didn't mean half he said?"

"No you didn't, Mary Waters. You thought the end of everything had come, even after I tried to convince you that it hadn't, and as for being glad, to be sure, I'm glad you've heard from your brother. Any one with relatives in the field must be very anxious."

"But you know, he said he was going to write to you, Nannie."

"It's very kind in him; I wonder he can take time from his Washington girls to write."

Then Mary laughed. "It can't be that you are jealous, Nannie, girl," she said affectionately taking her friend in her arms. "You know Tom is teasing you."

"I jealous!" oh how the little woman sniffed! "I can assure you that I'm not jealous, but I have the interests of my country at heart, and I cannot but feel sorry to see our soldiers giving themselves up to trivial amusements when she is in danger of—oh, just the most awful things. I'm not jealous, oh, no, but I'm ashamed of Tom."

"Why, Nannie, how can you?" said Mary reddening.

"Well, I am, and I mean it, and it's awful, that's what it is."

"I'm sorry my brother has offended you."

"Oh, Mary," Nannie was always inarticulate in her emotion, but Mary understood the burst of tears as Nannie threw herself on her bosom, and forgave her disparagement of Tom.

"What a little silly you are. You know he was only joking."

"Joking! Such a letter isn't any joke. It's brutal, that's what it is. Pretty girls cheering him! I hate those Washington girls. I just know they're bold, brazen things, and they didn't look at another man but Tom."

"Never you mind, you'll have a letter soon."

"I don't want it."

"All right. Maybe it won't come. The mails are very irregular now."

"Mary Waters, how can you say such a mean thing?"

"I didn't think you'd mind it."

"But I do mind it. You know the mails are regular here. It's not the mails that I'm worrying about."

She must have worried about something though, for when her father came in with the morning paper, she was eager to know if he had been to the post office, and on receiving a negative answer, was downcast for fully five minutes.

"The mail wouldn't have been sorted yet, anyhow," said her father, "and Banes's boy's going to bring it when he goes for theirs."

"The mail is very slow in Dorbury, isn't it?" Nannie proffered a little later, and was angry because Mary laughed again.

The promise of a letter was at least two days away, but Nannie ate very little that morning. She fastened her eyes upon the window which commanded the walk up which the Banes boy must come. Finally, when he hove in sight, she sprang away from the table with a cry, of "Oh, there he is!" and every one knew why her appetite had lapsed.

Fate was kind. It was kind two days ahead of promise, a strange thing, but this was her off day. There was a letter, and it was for Nannie and from Tom. She came directly to the table with it, because she didn't know any better, and there were no daws about to peck at an exposed heart. She read and smiled and bridled and blushed while the rest of the assembly neglected their eggs.

"Oh, give us some of it," said her father banteringly.

"I won't," she answered, and it was a good thing Tom couldn't see her smile and blush, for if he had been any sort of man, he would have deserted at once.

"Isn't there anything he says that we may hear?"

"Oh, do let me alone," she answered, and—well, it's hard to tell, but she giggled.

"What a softy he must be," said her little brother, "just writing about no-account things, when you'd think he'd be saying something about fighting. 'Tain't polite to read letters before folks anyhow."

"You hush up, Reuben," said Nannie indignantly, "don't you suppose a soldier can talk about anything but the horrors of war?"

"I knew it was from Tom," said Reuben jeeringly.

"Keep quiet, Reuben," said his father, "no telling when you'll be putting on fresh ties every night, an' tryin' to find out an excuse to be out to a 'literary' or a singing school."

Reuben grew red and was silent. His particular tone of red was what is denominated Turkey, and it was relieved by freckles.

"Well, I'll just read you a little of it," said Nannie finally. "I'm not going to tell you what he calls me in the beginning. That's none of their business, is it, Mary?" and she ran over and kissed Tom's sister for Tom's sake. Then she looked at the letter again.

"Well, he says, 'Dear little — ' no I'm going to leave that out. He sends his love to you, papa, but of course, that's at the last."

"Would it hurt you to be consecutive?" asked Nathan Woods drily.

"Oh, now, don't tease, just listen. He says, oh, Mary, he doesn't say another word about those Washington girls. It was only a joke, don't you think it was? I knew Tom couldn't be thinking very seriously just of girls when there was something very, very important to do. You know I told you so, Mary."

"No," said Mary tantalizingly, "I don't think that you did tell me just that."

"And of course," said her father, "you may not know it isn't, but this is not, I maintain, this is not hearing the letter."

"Oh, well, he says he's in Washington. How perfectly charming it must be in Washington. I know that must be a great town with the government and senators and such things about you. Dear, how I should like to be there, and oh, Mary, don't you remember about the Potomac in the geography, just think, Tom's seen the Potomac!"

"I know about the Potomac," said Reuben.

"That's not the letter yet," was her father's comment.

"Well, if you'd only stop, father, I'd get to it," said Nannie.

"We are dumb."

"Oh, papa, now, please don't joke, it's really very, very serious."

"Has one among them been taken?"

"That's just it, that's just it. The rebels tried to take them, and they didn't, and Tom—Tom—I think he ought to be promoted for it. It's wonderful."

"What did Tom do? Save his whole brigade?"

"Well, I don't know that he did that, but he says that he shot and shot, and that the bullets spit up against the car behind him. Think of it!"

"It would have been a good deal worse if they had spit up against him," said Woods. He had been in the Mexican war and unfortunately had lost his romance. "Now, daughter, for the letter."

"All right, you won't mind omissions, will you?"

"No, if you'll only omit your pauses and exclamations."

"'We are here, at last at the capital, and I tell you, it's a great place. I don't wonder in the least that men want to be congressmen when they can live in a town like this. Why, I'd be willing to take all the cares of the government on my shoulders just to live in a town like this. But you know, the voters have never pressed upon my shoulders the affairs of state, and so my willingness to be unselfish goes for nothing!' Now isn't that bright of Tom?"

"Oh, Nannie, for heaven's sake, go on." Nathan Woods was both short and impatient. "What we want is news, news about the troops and their condition there."

"I'm afraid, papa," said Nannie ruefully, "that there isn't much news. But never mind, listen. 'I got to see Lincoln the other day, and I don't think much of him. He's a big raw-boned fellow with a long face and an awfully serious look. But for any kind of polish I'll bet old Dennison could give him a good many lessons, although I don't think much of Dennison. My own——' Oh, no, there's where I've got to make an omission, but he goes on to say, 'People are saying that the rebellion is going to be a good deal bigger thing than we think, and that three months' service is hardly going to begin the fighting, others say different. Well, I don't care. I'm in it to stay, and you needn't expect to see me until we've licked the boots off these fellows. Do you know what they say? They boast that one Southerner can lick five Yankees.

Well, I'd like to see them try it.'   Oh, isn't that just like Tom?   He always was in for experiments."

"Go on, Nannie, and omit comment."

"'But as old man Wilson used to say in geometry class, if they proceed upon this hypothesis, they will be wrong.'   Oh, Mary, don't you remember old Mr. Wilson, and how often Tom used to tell us about his funny expressions.   How awfully clever of him to think of it now.   But I know you're waiting to hear the rest.   Oh, I can't read this, papa, not a bit of it.   Nor the rest, oh, I wouldn't read that for anything.   Tom is so enthusiastic.   You know how he is.   That's just what is going to make a good soldier out of him.   He says, 'I've seen General Schenck, and he's just what you would expect from the Schenck family.   It seems as if those people kept themselves busy making decent men.   The boys all like him, although they have not got generally trained into liking generals yet.   Say, Nannie —' and that's all," said the young girl with a guilty blush.

"How abruptly your brother ends his letters," said Nathan Woods, turning to Mary with a quizzical smile.   "It may be striking, but it's not a good literary style."

"You must always consider the collaborator, Mr. Woods," said Mary.

"In this case, I'm not sure that it has been collaboration. It may have been interpretation, or even, heaven help us, expurgation."

"Papa," said Nannie with a very red face, then she gathered up the loose sheets of her letter and fled from the table.

"Mary," said Nathan Woods, "what has happened this morning has made me very happy, but don't count too much upon it. No man respects your father more than I do. But the oyster opens his shell for a little and then shuts it as tight as ever. So I would advise you to stay with us a while longer. Had he wanted you at home, now this is plain, he would have come to you openly; but in putting the letter under the door, he only made a sacrifice on account of his love for Tom. Don't cry, little girl."

"No, I'm going to be brave, for I am glad even of this kindness from him—but —— "

"Aren't we treating you pretty well?"

"Yes, but Mr. Woods, you know, don't you?"

"Yes, I believe I do understand how you feel about it, but just keep on waitin', your time'll come."

CHAPTER XI

AT HOME

WITH the incidents that immediately succeeded the skirmish at Vienna, this story has little to do. Notwithstanding the enlistment of only three-months-men, the country had begun to settle down to the realization of war, not insurrection, not only rebellion any longer, but war, stern, implacable, and perhaps to last longer than had at first been expected. As the days passed, there was talk of reorganization. The first was not behindhand in the matter, and by the August following work among the men had begun.

On the day that the men came home, Dorbury, complacent because no casualty had as yet attacked her ranks, was out in full force to meet them. They, too, recognized the state of war, but as yet, it was only a passive condition, and when they saw their unbroken lines come back, three months' veterans, their pride and joy knew no bounds. That many of their men would return to the field, would go back to soldiers' deaths and soldiers' graves, did not disturb them then.

Sufficient into the day is the evil thereof. So they put away all thought of further disaster, and revelled only in the present.

Among those who came back, proud and happy, none was more noticeable than "Nigger Ed." The sight of camps, the hurry of men and the press of a real responsibility had evoked a subtle change in the negro, and though his black face showed its accustomed grins, and he answered with humor the sallies made at him, he capered no more in the public square for the delectation of the crowd that despised him. He walked with a more stately step and the people greeted him in more serious tones, as if his association with their soldiers, light though it had been, had brought him nearer to the manhood which they still refused to recognize in him.

Perhaps the least joyous of them all was Walter Stewart, who had given up his family for a principle. While the other boys returned to eager relatives, he came home to no waiting mother's arms, and no sweetheart was there to greet him with love and pride in her eyes. There were friends, of course, who gave him hearty hand-clasps. But what were friends compared with one's own family?

His mood was not improved when less than two days after the return there came a telegram calling him to the bedside of his dying father.

It was a great blow to the young fellow, and coming as it did, seemingly as a reproof of his career, it may be forgiven him, if in his grief, his heart grew lukewarm towards the cause he had espoused. As soon as he was able, he hastened away to Virginia and his father's bedside, torn with conflicting emotions of remorse, love and sorrow.

On an open space topping a hill near Dorbury, the white tents of the reorganizing regiment had begun to settle like a flock of gulls on a green sea. Most of the men who had been out were going back again, and the town took on a military appearance. It came to be now that the girl who had not a military lover or relative was one to be pitied, and the one who had, stood up with complacent Phariseeism and thanked her Creator that she was not as other maidens were.

It was now that the sewing-circle exerted itself to the utmost, both in their natural province and in entertainment for the soldiers. Everything now, had the military prefix to it. There were soldiers' balls, soldiers' teas, soldiers' dinners and soldiers' concerts. Indeed, the sentiment bade fair to run to a foolish craze, and those who felt most deeply and looked forward with fear to what the days might bring forth, beheld this tendency deprecatingly.

Many of the volunteers, from being decent, sensible fellows, had developed into conceited prigs. The pride of their families and the adulation of indiscreet women and none-two-well balanced men, combined to turn their thoughts more upon the picturesqueness of their own personalities than upon the seriousness of what was yet to be done. They were blinded by the glare of possible heroism, and sometimes lost sight of the main thing for which they had banded themselves together. It would be entirely false to say that at their first realization of what they had gone into they did not rise to all that was expected of them. But such was for a time the prevailing spirit, and for a while it called forth the sneers of old men who had not forgotten 1812 and 1846, at these three months' soldiers.

There were others, too, who smiled at the behavior of the young soldiers with less generous thoughts. Among them, Stephen Van Doren, who watched from behind closed blinds their comings and goings.

"Do they expect to whip the South, which is all fire and passion, with their stripling dandies, who go about the streets posing for a child's wonder and a woman's glance? Bah, the men who have gone into the field from the states of rebellion, have gone to fight for a principle, not to wear a uniform. They are all earnestness and self-sacrifice, and that's what's going to take the South to victory."

His old housekeeper, who was alone with him on the place, heard with admiration and belief, for she shared her master's opinion of the relative worth of the two sections of the country. Neither one of them knew that the young men of the South were taking their valets into the service with them; entering it as gallants with the traditionary ideas of the day, and leaving college for the field, because they believed it would be a famous lark.

It was perfectly true of both sections that neither looked upon the contest at first with a great amount of seriousness. But it is equally true that the fact might have been forgiven the youth of a country whose sons hitherto had made a common cause against a general enemy.

Unlike Van Doren, who stayed between walls and chuckled at the coming discomfiture of the Union arms, Bradford Waters was much upon the streets, and at Camp Corwin, as if the sight of these blue-coated defenders of the flag gave him courage and hope. He had a good word for every soldier he met, and his eyes sparkled as they told him of Tom, and the few experiences they had had together.

Tom, true to his promise, had not returned

with the rest, but had preferred to remain near the seat of war, and to join his regiment after its reorganization. The old man took pride, even, in this fact. To him, it was as if Tom were staying on the field where he could guard the safety of his country in an hour of laxity on the part of his comrades. He longed to see him, of course, but there was joy in the pain he felt at making a sacrifice of his own desires. He had not loaned his son to the cause. He had given him freely and fully.

The difference in attitude, between Van Doren and Waters, was the difference between regard for traditions and a personal faith. The Southerner said, "What my people have done," the Yankee, "What a man must do." Said one, "Coming from the stock he does, Bob must fight well." Said the other, "If they all fight like Tom, we're bound to whip." It all came to the same thing at last, but the contrast was very apparent then.

At news of the safety of his enemy's son, the copperhead had lost any sympathy he may have had for his Union antagonist, and the other no longer looked wistfully at his foreman's face when they chanced to meet.

It was not unnatural that the two girls, Nannie and Mary, should be affected by the hero-worshipping spirit of the town, and being deprived of the objects of their immediate affection, enter heartily into the business of spoiling all the other young men they could. To Nannie, it was all very pleasant, and something of coquetry entered into her treatment of the soldiers. But with Mary it was different. Her thoughts and motives were serious, and her chief aim was to do something for Tom's old associates, for Tom's sake.

There was no abatement of the rigor of the estrangement between her and her father, for although, after the incident of the letter, she had expected him to call her home, he had made no further sign, nor had she. She had yielded not one whit in her devotion and loyalty to Robert Van Doren. But she took pleasure in doing little kindnesses for the men whom she knew hated him for the choice he had made. The time soon came, when even this pleasure, gentle as it was, was denied her.

The story went round among the soldiers that old Waters' daughter was the sweetheart of a rebel soldier, and that in spite of all her good work, she had left home for love of him and his cause, and they grew cold towards her. Some were even rude.

It hurt the girl, but she continued her ministrations, nevertheless. Then one day as she passed through the camp where the girls sometimes went, she heard a voice from a tent singing derisively,

> "Father is a Unionist, so is Brother Tom,
>   But I, I'm making lots o' things
>   To keep a rebel warm."

Mary flushed and hurried on, but the voice sang after her:

> "Never mind my Union home, never mind my flag,
>   What's the glorious stars and stripes
>   Beside Jeff Davis' rag?
>   Damn my home and family, damn my Northern pride,
>   So you let me go my way to be a rebel's bride."

The song which some scalawag had improvised, cut Mary to the heart, but though no man would have dared sing it openly, she never took the chance of hearing it again. In spite of Nannie's pleadings, she would not go again where soldiers were congregated. Nor would she tell her reason, not that she felt shame in her love, but that there seemed some shade of truth in the song. She did want to go her way and she did want to be Robert's bride, even though they called him by such a name as rebel. She loved him and what had the stars and stripes or love of country to do with that? What he believed was nothing to her, it was only what he was.

She had heard from Robert but once since his departure; a brief but brave and loving letter, in which he told her that he was safe within the Confederate lines, and spoke of John Morgan, whom he had already begun to admire. Now in the dark moment of her sorrow, when every hand seemed turned against her because she loved this man, she dreamed over his letter as if it were a sacred writing, and so dreaming kept to herself whenever she could. Even old Nathan Woods began to look askance at her when her visits and ministrations to the soldiers ceased. But he comforted himself with the philosophy that "A woman is an unreasonable creature and never is responsible for her actions," and however false this may be in fact, it satisfied him towards Mary, and kept him unchanged to her. He was influenced, too, by Nannie's stalwart faith. While she could not understand Mary, could not enter into the secret chambers of her soul and see what was within there, she believed in her, and faith is stronger than knowledge.

"Never mind," she said one day after roundly scolding her friend for remaining so close to the house, " I know you've got some good reason, though I'm sure it's something fanciful. It's so like you, Mary." This may have been a bit inconsistent in the young girl, but it was expressive of her trust in Mary, and the burdened girl was grateful for it.

So, with bicker, prejudice, adulation, discon-

tent and a hundred other emotions that must
come to human beings, the stream of days went
on, and the reorganization of the First was an
accomplished fact. Still, from the South there
came news of battle and from Cincinnati there were
tidings of Kentucky's threatening attitude. West
Virginia had been rescued for the Union, but
what if this even more powerful state went over
to the Confederacy. Men were of many minds.
Some were wondering at the president for his
tardiness, and others cursing Dennison for his
rashness. It became the fashion to damn Lincoln on Sunday and Dennison on Monday. It
was from such a hot-bed of discontent that the
First finally tore itself, and left Dorbury on the
last day of October for the southernmost city of
the state.

CHAPTER XII

A JOURNEY SOUTH

THE condition of mind in which young Walter Stewart left Dorbury was not calculated to bring him back hastily for the reorganization of his old regiment. His thoughts were more of seeing his father alive, and of settling their differences, than of the righteousness of his cause. Indeed, as the train sped southward, his busy mind sometimes questioned if he had done right. If the North and South were one people as he claimed, would not neutrality have been the better course? Surely two brothers have the right to differ without the whole family's putting in. Is the love of country, which we call patriotism, a more commendable trait than filial affection and obedience, and can one deficient in the latter be fully capable of comprehending the former? Had he not by the very act of disobeying his father's wishes and refuting his wisdom in a case where right and wrong were so nearly related, demonstrated his inability for a high devotion and obedience to his country ? These, and like sophistries, raced through the young man's mind in the first heat of his remorse, and for the time, he forgot that his choice meant not less love for his father, but a broader devotion to his country. It was not for the sake of disobedience that he had cast his lot with the North, but in pursuance of an idea of a larger allegiance. But this he could not see, and as he worried and speculated, his distress grew.

When he reached Washington, he had anticipations of some difficulty in securing passage through the lines. There was every possibility of his being taken for a spy or an informer by one side or the other, and the fact that he was a lately mustered out soldier would make him an object of suspicion to both Unionist and Confederate. For the time being, his anxiety to be away, across the Potomac and into Virginia drove every other thought out of his head. Fortunately for him, he was known in Washington, and influential friends procured for him passes through the Union lines. His progress, after he reached the rebel outposts, was less speedy. But foreseeing this, he conceived that discretion would be the better part of valor, and so waited for night, and then the laxity of the few pickets scattered about helped him, and the stables of Falls Church were kind to him, and within an hour after darkness had fallen, he was galloping down the road towards Rockford.

The night was dark and the road none too even, but he rode as speedily as caution would allow. The way was unfamiliar to him, but he followed the directions he had received, trusting somewhat to the instincts of his horse to keep the path. Now and then, as the animal's hoofs clattered over the wooden bridge of river or streamlet, he held his breath lest he should rouse some lurking foeman. Once as he sped along a road besides which the trees grew thickly, a voice called to him to halt, but he only dug his spurs into the mare's flank, and leaning low over her neck, urged her on. Two shots spit vainly in the darkness as the road fell away under his horse's feet.

"Suppose I should miss the path," he said to himself, "and daylight find me still upon the way? Well, it's only a thing to chance now, and I must see father before he dies. I must see him!" The cry died away between clinched teeth, and leap after leap, the blackness swallowed him, and vomited him forth again. The branches of the trees underneath which he passed, reached out and caught at him as if they would detain him from his errand. The wind and the cricket and all the voices of the night called to him. The horse stumbled and her rider lurched forward, but the good steed was up and on again with scarcely a break in her pace, as if she knew that the man upon her back was crying in an agony of fear, " Father, father, live till I come ! "

As the distance lessened, Walter's mind was in a tumult of emotions. Again and again, the picture of his father already dead came before him. The white covering of the bed, the stark form and the weeping women all were vivid to him as actuality. He saw a light ahead of him, and checking the speed of his horse, he rode towards it. But he found that it came from a house up one of two roads which forked before him. He paused and looked helplessly at the diverging paths. He knew there was no time to be lost, and chafed at the delay. His indecision, however, did not last long. He turned the animal's head up the road on which the light was shining.

Proceeding cautiously, he found that the rays which had guided him came from the curtained, but unshuttered window of a little house standing back from the roadside, on a terrace. The place itself, did not look formidable, but there was no telling what elements of further delay were behind the closed door. Nevertheless, he reined in, and bringing his horse just inside the side gateway, hastened up the terrace and knocked at the door. There was the shuffling of feet within, and then the soft, swift scurrying as of some one hastening from the room. A moment later, the back door slammed, and a horse and rider clattered around the side of the house and out of the gate.

In spite of his haste and anxiety, Walter could but smile at the grim humor of the situation. That he, who stood there on the threshold, dreading what he should encounter beyond, should prove a source of terror to any one else, was but an illustration of the intermittent comedy which treads upon the heels of tragedy in the stern melodrama of war.

His reflections took but a moment; all that had passed, had hardly taken more time, but before the impressions were out of his mind, he found himself again knocking at the door.

"Who is there?" came a woman's voice.

"A stranger, but a friend."

"How do I know that you are a friend?"

"You need not know, you need not even open the door, only answer my question. I am hunting the house of Colonel Stewart, and am not sure that I am on the right road. Can you direct me?"

"You have missed your way," said the hidden woman in a voice that bespoke relief from some fear. "You should have taken the road to the right at the forks. The house is about two miles beyond on the right side. You can tell it without trouble. It is a large house, and there will be lights about it, for the colonel is very sick."

Walter did not wait to hear the woman's closing words, but with a hearty word of thanks, hurried away towards the gate. He was almost blithe with the thought that his journey would soon be over, and hope rose again in his heart. His father might be alive. He would be alive. He must be. So he went from hope to certainty as he passed with flying steps across the lawn and terrace to the gate. There he stopped with a gasp of alarm. His horse was no longer there. Gone, and the distance between him and his father lessened by many minutes when every second counted.

It all came to him in a flash. The frightened rider who had dashed away from the house in a flash, fearing pursuit, had taken the horse with him, or the animal, itself, had become frightened and followed involuntarily.

Walter halted hardly a moment, but turned swiftly back to the house. To his knock, came the woman's voice again in question.

"Some one has taken my horse," he cried.

"It is not so far to walk from here to Colonel Stewart's," said the woman coldly.

"But I cannot walk, I am pressed for time."

"I do not know you," was the reply, "nor do

I know your business, but I warn you that I am armed, and you had better go away."

"My God!" cried Walter, "I mean you no harm, but can't you help me to a horse, or must I take one wherever I can find it? I am Colonel Stewart's son, and my father is dying. I must see him." A dry sob broke in his throat.

An exclamation was uttered from within. Something that was very like the thud of a gun butt sounded on the carpeted floor. The bolts were shot and a woman stood in the flood of yellow light.

In the first instant, Walter saw the form of a tall young woman with fair hair, and behind her, the room disordered as by hasty movements. A gun stood against the wall. Further details he did not take note of.

"Come in for a moment," said the woman, "you need have no fear. I can help you to a horse." She was hastening into a wrap and hood as she spoke. "We already know of you, my brother and I; you are Colonel Stewart's Unionist son."

Walter flushed, but raised his head defiantly.

The young woman laughed as she hastened out of the room and came back with a lantern and key. "You need have no fear, there are no ambushes here. Come." She led the way around the house, where Walter could see the low outlines of the outbuildings.

"You gave us quite a fright; I may tell you, now that I know who you are. Brother is suspected of Unionist sentiments and has been looking to be arrested every moment. To-night, we took you for a Confederate officer, come to exercise that unpleasant commission, and it was he who must have frightened off your horse as he rode away. He's on Blue Grass, and if your horse keeps up with him, they're farther away now than you would care to follow."

During the last words she was unlocking the barn door. Then she handed the lantern to Walter, and called softly, "Come, Beth, come." A whinny answered her, and she went forward and quickly took the halter from a sleek brown mare. Walter started in to put the bridle on, but the girl waved her hand.

"No," she said, "I'll do it myself. Beth is my own particular pet, and is somewhat averse to strangers. You'll have to ride bareback too, as there isn't another man's saddle about. But she'll carry you safe when she's once on the road, and she'll turn in the right gate, for she knows the way."

The young man was stammering his thanks as the girl led the horse out. He would have walked with her back to the house, but upon an assurance that she was not afraid, he leaped to the mare's back and was off.

But it was not written that the object of his heart should be so easily obtained. He had scarcely gone half way to the crossroads, when the ominous word, "Halt!" sounded again in his ears, and several mounted men rose as from the road before him. Again, he gave spur to his horse, but this time, it was only for a moment that he moved, and then he came crash into another horseman, and felt the cold muzzle of a pistol pressed against his face, while a hand seized his bridle.

"Steady, my boy, steady, unless you want to get hurt. We don't want to do you any harm, but you mustn't move."

"Are you hurt, sergeant?" asked a voice from the darkness.

"No, cap'n, not particular. I may be a little strained, and this horse may be a little bruised up, but I was ready for the shock. I knew the youngster was game."

Just now the man addressed as captain rode up.

"Well, youngster," he said, "we've got a little business with you, and I reckon we're just in time."

Walter's head was whirling with the shock of his collision and he had a mean pain in the leg that had struck the other man's saddle. But he spoke up hotly.

"What's the meaning of this outrage?" he asked. "Cannot a man and a Virginian at that, ride his own roads in safety by night and by day?"

"Hoity-toity, not so fast, my young Union peacock, not so fast. Any Virginian may go his way in Virginia until he becomes dangerous to Virginia's cause. Then he comes with us as you do."

"What right have you to take me in this high-handed way?"

"We needn't bandy words, but I can say that we have the right that any state has to arrest within its borders any citizen who is suspected of working or attempting to work against its interest and safety. We have been watching you for a long time, Etheridge, and we know what your plans are."

They had been standing for the few moments that they talked, but now the company started to move off.

"Stop," cried Walter, as the name was called, "whom do you take me for?"

"We know who you are," said the captain grimly.

"But my name is not Etheridge, you are mistaken."

"What is this, sergeant?" asked the officer in charge of the party and who had done most of the talking.

"I know the horse, captain, it's his sister's."

"Come on, then, don't delay any further. It's no use denying your identity."

"But I can prove to you that I'm not the man you're seeking, nor is this horse mine. Having lost my own, I borrowed it at a house a little way up the road here."

"A very likely story."

"But if there is any one here who knows Etheridge, let him look at me and see."

The sergeant leaned forward and striking a match looked into Walter's face.

"Whew, captain," he whistled, "it's true, we've caught the wrong bird. This is not Nelson Etheridge. He's a stranger."

"Well, who the devil are you?" asked the captain shortly. "Strangers without credentials are not very welcome about here these times."

"My name is Walter Stewart, and my father is Colonel Stewart who lives about two miles from here."

"Stewart—Walter Stewart, hurrah, boys!" cried the captain, "we've lost one good bird but caged another! This is Colonel Stewart's Yankee soldier son. You'll do, come on."

"But, captain, I'm not in the service now, and

my father is dying. A few minutes' delay may keep me from ever seeing him alive."

"I am sorry," was the captain's reply, "but you have been a Union soldier. We take you leaving a suspected house, and find you as you tacitly admit within our lines and without credentials. It may be hard for you, but you are our prisoner."

"Very well, but cannot I be paroled at once? If necessary, send a soldier with me to my house, and keep me under guard."

The captain halted. "I know your father," he said coldly, "and he is a brave man and a Southern gentleman who has not forsaken the South. For his sake, I will do as you say, even though I exceed my authority. I will send two men with you. You will remain under guard until I secure your parole, if that may be done."

"I thank you," said Walter.

"Sergeant Davis!" The sergeant saluted.

"You and Private Wilkins will take charge of the prisoner. When his parole has been secured, you will be relieved. Until then, the closest vigilance."

"I am a soldier and a gentleman," said Walter calmly.

The officer vouchsafed no answer, but with his remaining associates spurred on into the darkness, leaving the prisoner to ride away with his captors.

CHAPTER XIII

As Walter approached his father's house, he saw lights moving about in the upper chambers, and he began to fear the worst.

"Have you heard any news of my father?" he asked the sergeant.

"None, except that he is a pretty sick man and not expected to last long."

"How did the captain and all of you come to know about me?"

"The servants will talk and it's few family secrets they don't know and tell. Your father invested in some niggers as soon as he got here in order to show his contempt for the Yankees' invasion, but they're too new to have any of the family pride that the old ones used to have. Why an old family servant would rather die than tell any of the happenings at the big house, but these darkies of your father's have blown his business broadcast."

Walter shivered at the man's tone and his revelations.

In order not to alarm the house unduly they dismounted at the gate and left the private to lead the horses around to the stables while the sergeant went with Walter. Their ring brought a servant to the door, who stood in white-eyed astonishment as he saw the young man, worn and haggard with anxiety and beside him, an officer in grey.

"W'y, w'y, gent'men, dis hyeah's a confede'ate house."

"Shut up and let us in. Make as little stir as possible, and bring my mother to the parlor. Sergeant, this will be a family meeting."

"You know my orders, sir."

"I do, and I am enough of a soldier not to want you to disobey them; but I prefer seeing my family alone. Examine the room where I shall talk with my mother, and have the places of egress guarded. I think the windows let out on a veranda."

"There may be more than one outlet, and I have not enough men to guard them if there is."

"You forget, sergeant," said Walter haughtily, "that I am a soldier and a gentleman."

"I'm not much of either yet," returned the non-commissioned officer calmly, "but I'm learning enough of a soldier's business to know how to obey orders."

"You are right," said the younger man blush-

ing. "Come, let's examine the room together
and see what dispositions we can make."

At this period, Private Wilkins came in from
his errand. They stationed him outside and
passed into the room. It was a large apartment,
with three long windows, opening, as Walter had
surmised, on the veranda.

"You see," pursued the sergeant, "it's just as
I said. You have too many places by which to
leave, though I do not doubt your honor."

"Let us see," said Walter going to the door.
"Ah, this will serve you," and he held up a key.
"Lock this door that shuts off one outlet. One
of you patrol the veranda and the other hold
the hall. Will that suit you?"

"Perfectly." And the sergeant proceeded to
do as directed. He stationed Wilkins in the
hall, and then as he was about to step out upon
the veranda, turned, and on a sudden impulse,
saluted the young private as if he were an officer.

He had hardly left the room, when Mrs.
Stewart came rushing in.

"Walter, Walter, my boy!"

"Dear little mother."

"Oh, you are well, you are well, aren't you?"

"In body, yes, mother, but—but—am I in
time?"

"Thank God, yes."

The young man bowed his head and the gesture itself, was a prayer of thanksgiving that God understood.

"I have so much that I want to say to you, mother, but take me to him at once. I am afraid that it will be too late. You shall have a talk with me afterwards." He put his arm affectionately about his mother's waist.

"Wait a moment, Walter," she said. "He is yet conscious. Oh, Walter, Walter, humor him, humor him in his dying moments. Promise, whatever he asks."

"Whatever he asks? Why, what can he ask?"

"Perhaps one great thing. Your father has not changed, even in the hands of death."

"I shall promise what I can without lying."

"If necessary, my son, lie, to ease your father's heart. Have I ever given you such advice before? Will you do it?"

He looked at her fondly for a moment, and then answered firmly, "I will lie, if need be. Take me to him."

They started out but Walter turned back to call the sergeant.

"I am going to my father's room," he said.

"I will come as far as the door," he said, "for the rest, I leave that to you. Go on."

As they passed up the broad steps, Mrs. Stewart asked in some agitation, "What does the presence of those soldiers mean?"

"Don't disturb yourself, mother, but I was taken on the way here after I had passed the reb —the Confederate lines, and I am a prisoner."

She grasped him by the arm. "A prisoner?" she gasped.

"Don't be alarmed," he went on soothingly, "I shall be paroled, the captain has as good as promised it, and then I shall be here with you."

"That is almost good," she replied, "and you will have less to promise."

The light was turned low in the sick room, and a nurse glided out as they entered. Walter's sister passed out also, and in passing pressed his hand.

Mrs. Stewart left her son at the door and went forward to the bed, a shadowy, gliding form in the dim room.

"Here is Walter," she said softly.

The sick man opened his eyes, and said weakly, but with some of his old coldness, "Raise the light, and let me see him."

"Father!" the boy stood over the bed.

The eyes that even then death was glazing, grew brighter as the colonel looked upon his son, but the words that he whispered huskily were, "Thank God, he does not wear their uniform. Walter!"

The young man threw his arms about his

father and held him close to his heaving breast. His eyes were tearless, but his bronzed face was pale and his throat throbbed convulsively. "Father, I am so sorry to have grieved you, so sorry."

"You're a Stewart," said the old man weakly, but dotingly. "They always were—they always were strong-headed. But you won't go back to them, will you, Walter? Will you? For your father's sake, for the sake of Virginia, you won't go back to the—Yankees?"

"I cannot lie to you, father, now," the filming eye formed a new light, and his mother started forward.

"What!"

"I could not go back to them if I would. I was taken on the way here, and am a prisoner in the hands of our own people."

The old man settled back with a glad sigh. "This is very good," he said, "very good. They can never have your services again. Better a prisoner in the camp of our people—our people —you said, Walter, than a general of those— aliens. Now I am content."

"Would you not better rest now?" asked his son gently.

"Yes, yes, I will rest," and he relaxed again upon his pillow.

Walter was easing his arms from underneath

the grey head, when the muscles of the dying man took on strength again. His eyes opened.

"Would you," he said almost fiercely, "would you go back to them again if you could?"

Walter cast one agonizing look at his mother's appealing eyes, then he answered firmly, "No, father, not if I could."

His father smiled. "I knew it," he murmured. "He is a Stewart, and a Stewart must come back to his own. Now I shall rest."

He sank into a soft slumber, and mother and son left the room on tiptoe.

"Come, you will go and see Emily now," said his mother.

"Let them come to my room," he said, "wherever you have placed me. We must make it as easy for Sergeant Davis as possible."

The morrow proved that the colonel had been right. He had rested, and the rest was one that should be eternally unbroken.

As soon as he found that the home was a place of death and mourning, the sergeant, be it said to his credit, relaxed some of his vigilance, and Walter was allowed to attend to the duties connected with his father's funeral with greater freedom. The same day, his parole was granted, and the house given over again to privacy.

In spite of a natural sorrow for his father's loss, Walter felt a sense of peace, even joy, at the reconciliation. The words, "Now I shall rest," rang in his head with soothing cadence. It was so much better this way than that his father should have gone from him in anger and reproach.

The joy Walter felt in coming back into the family circle proved how much his heart must have been hungering for it. Drawn by a strong enthusiasm for what he deemed the right, he had gone off into the wilderness to face death. But he had not ceased to look back with longing eyes towards the flesh-pots of Egypt. Being back to them, he was not prone to question why he came. The fact in itself, was sufficiently pregnant of content. Somehow, he did not feel ashamed of the satisfaction he felt in having the parole solve a vexing problem. He had lied to his father, had he not, in saying that he would not go back if he could? And then, he began to quibble with himself. Had he lied, after all? Was it not merely the premature assertion of a condition of mind that was to be? Would he go back if he could? He was not sure. His father had called him a Stewart, and that meant much. It was sweet to be there, with his own family, in the great old place. Going to the window, his eyes swept the surrounding landscape with restful satisfaction.

There was the broad sweep of lawn, and across

that, rugged against the sky, the dark row of outbuildings, the kitchen, the stables and the negro cabins, and beyond that, the woods. It was fine and manorial, and appealed to the something in Walter which is in every Anglo-Saxon, the love of pomp and circumstance and power. After all, it was for this he had been dragged from the camp and from the hardships of war, and was it not a pleasant change? Fate had been kind to him. There were many young fellows who would envy him, so why should he repine?

While he was still in the midst of his meditations, his mother came into the room.

" Brooding again ? " she said. " You must not do this, my son."

He blushed and raised his hand in protest, but his mother went on, " I know you were influenced by a strong principle, my son, a principle so deeply rooted that you were willing to give up everything for it, and you are longing to be back again. But yours are, after all, only the common fortunes of war."

The young man's face was burning, and all the thoughts that had just passed through his mind came surging back in an accusing flood. He saw that he had weakened on the side of his affections, and that for a little while he had put home and ease and mother-love before the cause for which he had once been so hot. His shame seethed in his face.

"You know what I told father," he said, "that I would not go back if I could?"

"Yes, yes, I know, and I understand what the falsehood cost you, but weighed against what it brought to your father and me, it seems justifiable. Why, Walter, don't you see that even a lie that softens a father's deathbed is a noble sacrifice?"

"I should feel the better if it were that way, but it is not a lie. It is coming to be true."

"Your heart is really coming over to the South?"

"Not to the South so much as to you and Emily and home and father's memory."

"Walter, Walter," she cried, embracing him, "this is nothing to hang your head about; this is true nobility!"

Her mother-love blinded her sight to his moral defection, but he saw and saw clearly, and was ashamed.

"It is strange," Mrs. Stewart mused, "how things have balanced. If the South has gained an adherent in you, the North has just taken one of Virginia's own sons."

"What do you mean?"

"The news came to us this morning that Nelson Etheridge has not returned, but has gone over to the Union lines."

"How do you know that?" cried Walter, starting up.

"We sent Cæsar with the horse this morning."

"Oh, I wanted to take it over myself and thank Miss Etheridge in person."

"You will have many chances to thank her," said his mother. "She is a great friend of Emily's and is often here."

"I am very glad," he stammered, "that is, on Emily's account."

When his mother left him, he too, went from the room, and sought the room where his father lay. He drew back the cloth and looked at the calm face, as stern and white as a figure in marble. Even in death, the lips had found their old line of compression, and the chin had not lost its decision.

"Oh, my father," said Walter, "I am a weaker man than you, but I am more your son than I knew." He replaced the cloth and went sadly away.

The funeral of Colonel Stewart was a piteous affair. The remnants of the families about came to pay their respects to the dead. But mostly, they were women or old men. The army had taken the rest. The clergyman who conducted the services wore the grey under his gown, and as soon as his work was done, left his vestments and rode back to the regiment of which he was chaplain.

People looked askance at Walter or did not look at him at all. To them, he had the shame of being a Unionist on parole, but within him there was a greater shame—that he was neither with them nor against them.

CHAPTER XIV

THE CONTRABANDS

IT was now that a new unpleasantness began to harass the already burdened people of Ohio. The decree of General Butler making all slaves who came into camp contraband of war, affected the negroes not only in his immediate vicinity, but wherever there was a Union camp. Drunk with the dream of freedom, at the first intimation of immunity, they hastened to throw off their shackles and strike for the long-coveted liberty. Women, children, young, able-bodied men and the feeble and infirm, all hastened towards the Union lines. Thence, it was usually an easy matter, or at least, one possible of accomplishment, to work their way North to the free states.

Hardly a camp, hardly a column in which the officers were not reputed vigorously to oppose the admission of slaves but presented a strange and varied appearance. In the rear, but keeping close to their saviors always, straggled a lot of half-clad, eager negroes of all ages and conditions, bearing every conceivable form of movable property—bags, bundles, bedclothes, cooking utensils, and even an occasional calf or sheep trailed along. Many, indeed, found employment as the servants of officers, where their traditional qualifications as cooks or valets came into full play. But for the most part, they simply hung on, worrying and embarrassing the soldiers with their importunities, sickening and dying from fatigue and exposure, and conducting themselves altogether, like the great, helpless, irresponsible children that they were.

To those, who only a few years ago, primed with the prejudices of their masters, had looked upon the Yankees as monsters, there had come a great change, and every man who wore the blue had become as God's own vicegerent. They had been told that the Yankees had horns, and many of them believed it, but on contact, the only horn that they had found was the horn of plenty, and their old faith in their masters' infallibility died.

They were not all a burden, though. In the gloom of the dark hours, their light-heartedness cheered on the march; their pranks, their hymns and their ditties made life and light. Through the still watches of the night, the lonely sentinel on his beat, heard their singing and sometimes he thought of home with a choking at his throat, and had a vision of a tender mother singing to the babe upon her breast, and he looked up to the stars, and was alone no more.

The poor blacks, wandering in the darkness of their ignorance were as frightened children in the night. They had lost faith in their masters, but it was not lost to them entire, only transferred to these new beings, who mastered them by the power of love. Is it any wonder that they shouted and sang, and that often their songs were "Out of Old Egypt," "De Promised Lan'," and "Go Down Moses"?

One of the principal songs they sang, ran thus, a low minor melody at first, then breaking in the improvisation into a joyous shout:

> "In Egypt I sang a moun'ful song,
>   Oh, Lawd, de life was ha'd;
> Dey said yo' bondage won't be long,
>   Oh, Lawd, de life was ha'd.
> Dey preached an' dey prayed, but de time went on,
>   Oh, Lawd, de life was ha'd;
> De night was black w'en dey talked of dawn,
>   Oh, Lawd, de life was ha'd:
> We t'ought 'twas day in de lightin' flash,
>   Oh, Lawd, de life was ha'd,
> But night come down wid de mastah's lash,
>   Oh, Lawd, de life was ha'd."

And, then, some clear voice would break into further improvisation,

> " But de Yankees come and dey set us free,
>   T'ank Gawd, hit's bettah now,

De Yankee man is de man fu' me,
  T'ank Gawd, hit's bettah now —
He gi' me braid an' he gi' me meat,
  T'ank Gawd, hit's bettah now,
Eatin' nevah did seem so sweet,
  T'ank Gawd, hit's bettah now.''

For them it was better now, though they toiled and struggled and fell by the wayside. The abstract idea of freedom which they did not yet understand, had become a fetich to them. And over the burning sands, or through the winter's snow where they trudged with bleeding feet, they kept their stalwart faith in it. They were free at last, and being free, no evil thing could hurt them.

It was strange that most of them should not have become discouraged and gone back to the fleshpots still in Egypt. The Union officers did not understand these great children who flocked so insistently about their heels. Some were harsh to them, and others who would have been kind, did not know how. But they staid on and on, clinging to the garments of the army, going from camp to camp, until they swept like a plague of locusts into some Northern town.

Ohio, placed as she was, just on the border of the slave territory, was getting more than her share of this unwelcome population, and her white citizens soon began to chafe at it. Was their free soil to become the haven for escaped negroes? Was this to be the stopping ground for every runaway black from the South? Would they not become a menace to the public safety? Would they not become a public charge and sorely strain that generosity that was needed to encourage and aid the soldiers in the field? These and a thousand such conjectures and questions were rife about the hapless blacks. The whole gamut of argument that had been used in '49, '50 and '51 was run again. The menace of Maryland with her free negroes was again held up. The cry rose for the enforcement of the law for the restriction of emancipated negroes, while others went to the extreme of crying for the expulsion of all blacks from the state.

Since 1829, there had been a gradual change for the better in the attitude of Ohio towards her colored citizens, but now, all over the state, and especially in the southern counties and towns there had come a sudden revulsion of feeling, and the people rose generally against the possibility of being overwhelmed by an influx of runaway slaves. Their temper grew and ominous mutterings were heard on every side. The first great outburst of popular wrath came when negro men began offering themselves for military service, and some extremists urged the policy of accepting them.

"Take them," said the extremists, "and you break the backbone of the South's power. While the Southern men are in the field, fighting against the government their negro slaves are at home raising supplies for them, and caring for their families. When we enlist them, whom have they to leave for such duties?"

But all the North held up its hands and cried, "What, put black men beside our boys to fight? Let slaves share with them the honor and glory of military service? Never!"

The army itself hurled back its protest, "We are fighting for the Union; we are not fighting for niggers, and we will not fight with them."

From none of the states came a more pronounced refusal than from Ohio. She had set her face against men of color. What wonder then, that their coming into the state aroused all her antagonistic blood? Here, for the time, all party lines fell away, and all the people were united in one cause—resistance to the invasion of the black horde. It was at this time that Butler's proclamation struck through the turmoil like a thunderbolt, and the word "Contraband" became a menace to the whites and a reproach to the blacks.

The free blacks of Dorbury themselves, took it up, and even before they could pronounce the word that disgusted them, they were fighting their unfortunate brothers of the South as vigorously as their white neighbors. "Contraband" became the fighting banter for black people in Ohio. But the stream kept pouring in. In spite of resistance, abuse and oppression, there was a certain calm determination about these fugitive slaves that was of the stuff that made the Puritans. As far North as Oberlin and Cleveland, they did not often make their way. If it was their intention to stop in Ohio at all, they usually ended their journey at the more Southern towns. While the spirit in the Northern towns was calmer, it was, perhaps, just as well that they were not overrun. In Cleveland, especially, numerous masters of the south, averse to making slaves of their own offspring, had colonized their discarded negro mistresses and their illegitimate offspring, and these people, blinded by God knows what idea of their own position, in the eyes of the world, had made an aristocracy of their own shame.

In Dorbury, the negro aristocracy was not one founded upon mixed blood, but upon free birth or manumission before the war. Even the church, whose broad wings are supposed to cover all sorts and conditions of men, turned its face against the poor children of a later bondage.

After much difficulty, the negro contingent in Dorbury had succeeded in establishing a small house of worship in an isolated section known as "the commons." Here, according to their own views, they met Sunday after Sunday to give praise and adoration to the God whom they, as well as the whites, claimed as theirs, and hither, impelled by the religious instincts of their race, came the contrabands on reaching the town. But were they received with open arms? No, the God that fostered black and white alike, rich and poor, was not known to father these poor fugitives, so lately out of bondage. The holy portals were closed in their faces, and dark-skinned pastors, not yet able to put the "H" in the educational shibboleth, drew aside their robes as they passed them.

Opposition was even expressed to their fellowship with the Christian body. It reached its height when, on a memorable Sunday—a quarterly meeting day in fact, three families of the despised, presented themselves for membership in the Wesleyan chapel. The spirit had been running high that day, and there had been much shouting and praising the Lord for his goodness. But at this act of innocent audacity, the whole tone of the meeting changed. From violent joy, it became one of equally violent anger and contempt. These outcast families seeking God, had stepped upon the purple robes of these black aristocrats, and they were as one for defiance.

One aged woman, trembling with anger and religious excitement, tottered up, and, starting for the door, hurled this brief condemnation of the culprits who dared desire membership in her church: "W'y, befo' I'd see dis chu'ch, dis chu'ch dat we free people built give up to dese conterbands, I'd see hit to' down, brick by brick."

She hurried down the stairs, and a number followed her. But some stayed to remonstrate with the unreasoning contrabands. They were told to form a church of their own and to worship together.

"But," said their spokesman, who had preached down on the plantation, "whyn't we jes' ez well wo'ship wid you? We's all colo'ed togethah."

The pastor tried in vain to show them the difference between people who had been freed three or four years before and those just made free, but somehow, the contraband and none of his company could see it, and the meeting was broken up. The rejected Christians, seeking their poor shanties in amazement, and the aristocrats gathering to talk among themselves over the invasion of their temple.

With both white and black against them, it could not be long before the bad feeling against these poor people must break out into open attack. Theirs was a helpless condition, but they were not entirely alone. In all the town, they had no stronger friend than Stephen Van Doren. A Southerner by birth and education, he understood these people, who had for two centuries been the particular wards of the South. While he had no faith in the ultimate success of the Union arms, and believed that all these blacks must eventually go back into slavery whence they had come, yet he reasoned that they were there, and such being the case, all that was possible, ought to be done for them.

The negroes were quick to recognize a friend, and his house soon became the court to which they took all their grievances. He had been keeping indoors, but now he began to circulate among his Southern friends, and to do what he could to help his poor protégés.

It was then that the first inklings of a contemplated attack upon them came to his ears. Some of the citizens of Dorbury, inspired by the public spirit which barroom speeches arouse, had determined to rise and throw off the stigma of negro invasion. The embers of the people's passions had long smouldered, and when a pseudo-politician in the glow of drink had advised them to rise and drive the black plague beyond their borders, they had determined to do so.

The conduct of the whole matter had been put into the hands of Raymond Stothard, for the politician declined to lead such an assault, upon the plea that it was hardly the proper thing for a man who aspired to the legislature.

Stothard was chosen, first, because he was the brother of the prosecuting attorney, which would give the movement prestige, and next, because he was capable of doing anything when he was drunk. He usually was drunk or becoming so. He was drunk when he made the speech which instantly made him the leader of the aggressive movement.

"Gen'lemen," he said, "you all know me, and you know that I ain't the man to try to lead you into an unjust fight, now am I?" He was almost plaintive and the crowd about him cried, "No, no!"

"Thank you," he went on, swaying at his table. "Thanks, I'm glad to see that you per—preciate my motives. You all know my brother, he's a straight—straight man, ain't he? You all know Philip Stothard. Now I'm a peaceable man, I am. But to-night, I say our rights and liberties are being invaded, that's what they are. All the niggers in the South are crowding in on us, and pretty soon, we won't have a place to lay our heads. They'll undercharge the laborer and drive him out of house and home. They will live on leavings, and the men who are eating white bread and butter will have to get down to the level of these black hounds.

"I don't like 'em, anyhow. None of us like 'em. The whole war is on their account. If it hadn't been for them, we'd have been friends with the South to-day, but they've estranged us from our brothers, rent the country asunder, and now they're coming up here to crowd us out of our towns. Gentlemen, I won't say any more. It shall never be said that Ray Stothard was instrumental in beginning a revolt against law and order. My brother's prosecuting attorney, you know, and we stand for the integrity of the law. But if I had my way, I'd take force, and clear this town of every nigger in it. Gentlemen, drink with me."

His final remark was the most eloquent plea he could have made. The gentlemen drank with Mr. Stothard and voted his plan for saving their homes and workshops a good one.

One man in passing had heard the sound of speechmaking within, and out of idle curiosity had paused at the saloon door in time to hear Stothard's stirring remarks. Stephen Van Doren listened with horror to what the drunken rowdy proposed, and then went with all speed to his brother.

"You're too sensible a man, Van Doren," said the prosecuting attorney, "to believe that I have anything to do with this matter or would countenance it. But I can do nothing whatever with this brother of mine; there is only one thing to do, and that is to warn the negroes."

"They are not used to fighting for themselves. They would be as helpless as children and could be killed like sheep in a pen."

"They have their freedom, taken as you and I both believe, illegally, let them rise to the occasion which liberty demands," and so the lawyer dismissed the subject, although Van Doren gave back the answer that what these blacks had to meet was not the result of liberty, but the mockery·of it.

Leaving Philip Stothard's house, Stephen Van Doren went his way, torn between conflicting opinions as to his duty. Would he be proving a traitor to his fellow-citizens if he told the negroes of the designs against them? But were these men of the lowest social stratum, loafers, ignoramuses and fanatics his fellow-citizens? Was it not right that these poor fellows, slaves as they had been, and would be again doubtless, should be allowed the chance of defending themselves against assault? He argued with himself long and deeply that night, and in the end he decided that the blacks must be warned. He did not know when the attack would take place. Indeed, he felt sure that it would wait upon inspiration and opportunity, but the intended victims could be put upon their guard and then be left to look out themselves. He could do no more. Perhaps he had already done too much.

On the morrow, he saw some of the blacks, and after cautioning them to secrecy as to what they should hear, told them of their danger. They heard him with horror and lamentation They were bitterly disappointed. Was this the freedom for which they had toiled ? Was this the welcome they received from a free state ? They already knew how the church had greeted them. But they were the more shocked because they found out for the first time that politics could be as hard as religion.

One advantage which the negroes were to have was that in the sudden passion against their race the whites made no distinction as to bond or free, manumitted or contraband. This, of necessity, drew them all together, and they grew closer to each other in sympathy than they had yet known.

The drawing together was not one of spirit only, but of fact. They began to have meetings at night after the warning, and a code of signals was arranged to call all of them together at the first sign of danger.

Meanwhile, Stothard and his confederates, believing that all their workings had been done in profoundest secrecy, only waited an opportunity to strike effectively and finally.

The leader's first open act occurred one day when he seemed to have found an audience of sympathizers. He was strolling along busy with his usual employment of doing nothing, when he noticed a crowd gathered at a point upon the street that led from the railway station. He sauntered towards it, but quickened his pace when he found that the centre of the group was a small family of black folk who had just arrived from some place south of the river. There were a father and mother, both verging on old age, a stalwart, strong-limbed son, apparently about twenty, and two younger children. They were all ragged, barefoot and unkempt. They had paused to inquire the way to the negro portion of the town, and immediately the people, some with animosity, some with amusement, had gathered around them.

"What's all this?" asked the attorney's brother, as he reached the group. None of the whites vouchsafed him an answer, and he turned his attention to the negroes.

"More niggers," he exclaimed. "Why in hell don't you people stay where you belong?"

The blacks eyed him in silence.

"Why don't you answer when I talk to you?" He took a step forward, and the outcasts cowered before him, all save the son. He did not move a step and there was a light in his eye that was not good to see. It was the glare of an animal brought to bay. Stothard saw it and advanced no further, but went on.

"If I had you across the line, I'd teach you manners." The old woman began to cry.

"We come up hyeah," said the young negro, "'cause we hyeahed it was a free state."

"It's free for white people, not for niggers."

"We hyeahed it was free fu' evahbody, dat's de reason we come, me an' mammy an' pappy an' de chillun. We ain't a bothahin' nobody. We jes' wants to fin' some of ouah own people."

"There's enough of your people here now, and too many, and we don't want any more. You'd better go back where you come from."

"We cain't go back thaih. Hit's been a long ways a comin', an' we's 'bout wo' out."

"That's none of our business; back you go. Gentlemen, unless we put our foot down now, we shall be overrun by these people. I call you to act now. Turn them back at the portals of the city. Ohio as a state and Dorbury as a town does not want these vagabonds."

Unseen by Stothard, another man attracted by the gathering had joined the crowd, and now his voice broke the silence. "Who made you, Ray Stothard, the spokesman for the people of Ohio?"

The aristocratic loafer turned to meet the eye

of Stephen Van Doren, and his face went red in a second.

"I don't know what right you've got to speak, Van Doren, you've done everything you could to hurt the Union."

"It is to the Union's greatest discredit that it has such men as you on its side."

"So you're in favor of letting the niggers over-run the town?"

"I'm in favor of fair play, and I intend to help these people find their fellows."

"Humph, what are you anyhow? First a copperhead, then a rebel, then the champion of contrabands. You're neither fish, flesh, fowl nor good red herring."

"Whatever I may be, I'm not a conspirator." Stothard blanched at the word. "Nor," went on the old man, "am I a barroom orator and leader of ruffians. Come, boys," he said address-ing the negroes, and they grinned broadly and hopefully at the familiar conduct and manner of address of the South which they knew and loved. Away they went behind Van Doren.

"Go on, Steve Van Doren," Stothard crowed after the old man like a vanquished cock. "But you may have more work to do before you get through with your nigger pets."

"All right," was the sturdy answer. "When-ever you and your hounds come for me, you'll find me waiting, and by heaven, you'll leave me weightier men by a few ounces than you've ever been before."

The younger man attempted to raise a jeer as the other man passed down the street. But the crowd refused to join him. There was something too majestic in the carriage of the old copperhead. He commanded an inevitable, if reluctant respect. The same independent habit of thought and sturdy disregard of consequences that made him a copperhead, made him a friend to these poor helpless blacks.

Stothard, however, was not done. He was inflamed with anger at his defeat and the shame put upon him. He hurriedly left the crowd, and went at once to the rendezvous of his confederates. All that day and night he harangued them as they came in one by one, setting before them the alleged dangers of the case, and painting the affair of the afternoon in lurid colors. By midnight, drunken men who mistook intoxication for patriotism, talked solemnly to each other of the "Black invasion," and shook hands in the unity of determination to resent this attack upon the dignity of the state.

All the next day there was an ominous quiet in Dorbury. Men who had no other occupation than lounging about the courthouse corner and in the barrooms were not to be seen. There were no violent harangues in the livery stables and groceries. Mr. Raymond Stothard was not out.

About dusk the clans began to gather. One by one they came from their holes and hiding-places and made their way to the rendezvous. Over their drinks, they talked in whispers and the gaslight flared on drawn, swollen, terrible faces. Their general had found the wherewithal to buy liquor and he plied them well.

Meanwhile on old McLean street, where stood the house of one of Dorbury's free black citizens another gathering equally silent, equally stealthy and determined was taking place. The signal had gone forth, the warning had been received and free negro and contraband were drawing together for mutual protection. Not a word was spoken among them. It was not the time for talk. But they huddled together in the half-lit room and only their hard, labored breathing broke the silence. To the freemen, it meant the maintenance of all that they had won by quiet industry. To the contrabands, it meant the life or death of all their hopes of manhood. Now all artificial lines were broken down, and all of them were brothers by the tie of necessity. Contraband and the man who a few days ago had looked down upon him with supreme contempt, now pressed shoulder to shoulder a common greyness in their faces, the same black dread in their hearts. In the back room sick with fear, waited the women and children. Upon the issue of the night depended all that they had prayed for. Was it to be peace and home or exile and slavery? Their mother hearts yearned over the children who clustered helpless about their feet. "If not for us, God, for these, our little ones," they prayed. Their minds went back to the plantation, its pleasures and its pains. They remembered all. There had been the dances and the frolics, and the meetings, but these paled into insignificance before the memory of the field, the overseer and the lash. Often, oh, too often, they had bared their backs to the cruel thongs. Day by day they had toiled and sweated under the relentless sun. But must these, the products of their poor bodies, do likewise? Must they too, toil without respite, and labor without reward? They clasped their children in their arms with a hopelessness that was almost aggression.

The little black babies that night did not know why their mothers hugged them with such terrible intensity or hushed them with such fierce tenderness when they cried.

It was nearly midnight when the whisper ran round the circle in the front room, "They are coming, they are coming!" and the men drew themselves closer together. The sound of the shuffling of many feet and the noisy song of a drunken mob awoke the echoes of the quiet street. Then, of a sudden, the songs ceased as if some authoritative voice had compelled silence. Nearer and nearer moved the feet, softer now, but with drunken uncertainty. They paused at the gate. The lock clicked. The men within the room were tense as bended steel. Then came a thunderous knock at the door. No answer.

There was a pause, and apparently a silent conference. The rioters had sought several other suspected houses, the chapel among them, and found them empty. Here then, was the place which they had definitely settled as the negroes' stronghold.

"Open in the name of the law," came a voice.

The blacks huddled closer together. Then came a blow upon the door as from the stock of a gun.

"Gently," said the voice, "gently." But the spirit of violence having once been given rein could not be controlled, and blow after blow rained upon the none too strong door, until it yielded and fell in with a crash. But here, the mob found themselves confronted by a surprise. Instead of a cowering crowd of helpless men, they found themselves confronted by a solid black wall of desperate men who stood their ground and fought like soldiers. At first, it was fist, stave, club and the swift, silent knife, and only the gasp of forced breath and the groan of some fallen man told that the terrible fight went on. Then a solitary shot rang out, and the fusillade began. The blacks began to retreat, because they had few weapons, putting their women-folks behind them. Gradually, the white horde poured into the room and filled it.

"Now, boys," said Stothard's voice from the rear, "rush them!" and he sprang forward. But a black face confronted him, its features distorted and its eyes blazing. It was the face of the contraband boy whom he had abused the day before. A knife flashed in the dim light, and in a moment more was buried in the leader's heart. The shriek, half of fear, half of surprise which was on his lips, died there, and he fell forward with a groan, while the black man sped from the room. The wild-eyed boy who went out into the night to be lost forever, killed Stothard, not because he was fighting for a principle, but because the white man had made his mother cry the day before. His ideas were still primitive.

The rout of the negroes was now complete, and they fled in all directions. Some ran away, only to return when the storm had passed; others, terrified by the horror of the night, went, never to return, and their homes are occupied in Dorbury to-day by the men who drove them from them.

The whites, too, had had enough, and their leader being killed, they slunk away with his body into the night which befriended them.

CHAPTER XV

In the days that ensued after the mustering out of Tom's regiment neither he nor Dorbury had time for idleness. The events attending the conflict both in the field and at home had followed each other too swiftly for that. Tom had found military service under the government in a capacity that gave him larger experience in the world of men. His letters had given his father exceeding joy and Mary and Nannie were inordinately proud of him. His messages to them were read over and over again as the girls prepared themselves for sleep or sat half-robed upon their bedsides.

The gossips had still spared the brother the story of the breaking up of his home and he went on with his work happy in his unconsciousness. When the final reorganization of the First took place in November, he relinquished his other duties and joined his comrades at Louisville, whence they set out on their journey further South.

In the meantime, Dorbury had continued to seethe as before, with the conflicting elements within its narrow borders. Patriotism and prejudice ran riot side by side, and it was a hard race between them. One set of men talked of the glory of righteous war, while another deplored the shedding of fraternal blood. The war Republicans hurled invectives at the peace advocates, and the latter hurled back invectives and reproaches.

Before the First went back into the field an incident occurred which showed the temper of both parties. A meeting was being held in the square in front of the courthouse. Its object was to protest against what the opponents of the war called the attempted coercion of free citizens. Mr. Vallandigham, whose position, both as a prominent citizen and former congressman gave weight to whatever he said, had spoken and the hearts of his hearers were inflamed with bitterness. Another speaker, half-hearted and little trusted rose to address the assembly. He was a fiery demagogue and depended for his influence upon his power to work upon the passions of the lower element. His audience knew this. He knew it, and for an instant, paused in embarrassment.

Just at that moment, "Nigger Ed" strolled up and joined the crowd. The eye of the orator took him in, and lighted with sudden inspiration. Here was all the text he needed. Raising his tall, spare form, he pointed in silence until every face was turned upon the negro. Then he said, "Gentlemen, it is for such as that and worse that you are shedding your brothers' blood." Without another word, he sat down. It was the most convincing speech he had ever made. The unhappy advent of the negro had put a power into the words of a man who otherwise would have been impotent. It was the occasion and the man to take advantage of it. It may have been clap-trap. But in the heated spirit of the time, it was a shot that went straight to the mark. The crowd began to murmur and then broke into hisses and jeers. Rude jests with more of anger than humor in them were bandied back and forth.

One side was furious that blood should be spilled for such as the negro bell-ringer, while the other was equally incensed at being accused of championing his cause.

"Nigger-stealers! Abolitionists!" shouted one.

"Copperheads!" shouted the other, while some of them tried fruitlessly to explain that they had no interest in niggers.

"He even wears your army cap!" some one cried. "Why don't you give him a gun?"

The stentorian voice of Bradford Waters rose

over the storm. " Your friends, the rebels," he said, " have got the niggers digging trenches, and tilling the fields at home to help them in food."

" Ah, that's their business," was the reply.

"I don't know that a gun is any better than a spade."

Back and forth the controversy raged, each party growing hotter and hotter. Negro Ed stood transfixed at the tempest he had raised. He looked from face to face but in none of them found a friend. Both sides hated him and his people. He was like a shuttlecock. He was a reproach to one and an insult to the other.

" Gent'men, gent'men," he began to stammer to the men about him who were hustling him.

" Knock him down, he's been serving the men who fought our brothers."

" Tear off his cap, the black hound, it's the same our soldiers wear."

" Kill him; if it wasn't for his kind, we'd have had no trouble ! "

" What's he doing here, anyhow ? This is a white man's Union. Down with niggers ! "

And so the bewildered black man was like to be roughly handled by both parties, but that an opportune interruption occurred. The gavel sounded sharp and harsh and some one was speaking.

" Let Ed alone," the speaker said. " He has done nothing to you. He has rung our bells, followed our fires, amused our children and always been harmless."

The crowd began to remember that all this was true.

" He is not his people, nor the father of them. The trouble is not with him but with us. It's not without, it's within. It's not what he is but what we believe."

Stephen Van Doren's voice had arrested the activities of the mob and they gave him absolute attention. In the respite, the negro, glad of his release, slipped away with the insulted cap in his hand. What he felt is hardly worth recording. He was so near the animal in the estimation of his fellows (perhaps too near in reality) that he could be presumed to have really few mental impressions. He was frightened, yes. He was hurt, too. But no one would have given him credit for that much of human feeling. They had kicked a dog and the dog had gone away. That was all. Yet Ed was not all the dog. His feeling was that of a child who has tried to be good and been misunderstood. He should not have felt so, though, for he knew Dorbury and the times by an instinct that was truer than conscious analysis, and he should have known, if he did not, that the people who mistreated him, were not sane and accountable. But the under dog does not stop to philosophize about his position. So Ed went his way in anger and in sorrow.

After Van Doren's interruption, the meeting went on in a somewhat more moderate strain, though the speeches that were made were bitter enough. A new, but vigorous and efficient governor was in the chair, and at times the people chafed under the enforcement of measures which, in a state of war, he deemed necessary. No great disaster had yet come to their own troops to unite the people in one compact body, or to make them look farther than themselves or their fancied personal grievances. The sight of the wounded and the news of the dead had not yet thrilled them into the spirit for self-sacrifice. This was to come later. It was to come when the soil of the state was threatened by hostile invasion; when Pittsburg Landing had told its bloody story, and the gloom of death hung over their homes.

But now all was different. After the first enthusiasm for war had passed, a reaction had set in. Recruiting went on slowly, while the citizens looked on with but languid interest. On the other hand, they flamed with anger at every hint that their personal rights were being trampled on. When men, lacking both honor and loyalty, wrote seditious letters; when others, more earnest than prudent, talked in the public highways or harangued from platforms, it was all free speech, the fetich so dear to American worshippers, and they resented any attempt to restrain or abridge it.

A man might live and work under the flag whose soldiers he counselled to desert. That was all within his private right. Another might assail the motives and powers of the government under which he lived, sneer at its chief executive, and pour out the vials of his wrath against the unholy war which the Union was waging, and still, it was only his right. Any attempt to check disaffection within its borders was construed into coercion. Where now and then, some too bold speaker was arrested by the authorities, war Democrat, and peace Democrat united in denouncing the act as high-handed and unwarranted, and Republican joined with them or was silent.

Upon one thing they were all united, and that was their hatred and disdain for the hapless race which had caused the war. Upon its shoulders fell all the resentment and each individual stood for his race. If their boys suffered hardships in the field, they felt that in some manner they avenged them by firing a negro's home or chasing him along the dark streets as he made his way home from church. It became an act of patriotism to push a black woman from the sidewalks.

It only needed the knowledge that free men of color had offered their services to the state to bring out a storm of invective and abuse against the "impudent niggers." There were some who expressed fear that the governor might yield to their plea, and threatened if he did, that they would call their sons and brothers from the army, and resent the insult by withholding all aid from the Union arms. But they need have had no fear of their governor. Strong as he was and independent, he was too wise a man not to know and to respect the trend of popular sentiment, and he heard with unyielding heart the prayer of the negroes to be put in the blue. But the time did come when the despised race was emancipated and they were accepted in the field as something other than scullions. The time came, yes, but this governor was not one of the men who helped to hasten it. It may have been his personal feeling, rather than his acquiescence to the will of the people that prompted his reply to the Massachusetts recruiting agent. The New England commonwealth was recruiting her black regiments and was drawing men of color from every state. When the chief executive of Ohio was consulted, he was so far from objecting to the use of his negroes by another state that he expressed himself to the effect that he would be glad if they would take " every damned nigger out of the state." It may have been irritation at the anxiety and annoyance that this unwelcome population had caused the good governor which brought forth this strong expression. Whether it was this or not, the fact remains that many black men of Ohio went into the Massachusetts regiments, and when they had made for themselves a record that shamed contempt, it was to that state that popular belief gave the honor of their deeds.

This forecasting of events would be entirely out of place but that it serves in some manner to show the spirit of the times in a loyal and non-slaveholding state at a crucial moment of the nation's life; it was a moment when only a spark was needed to light the whole magazine of discontent and blow doubt and vacillation into a conflagration of disloyalty.

The spark was near being supplied on a Monday night in May. Upon the flint of Dorbury's public pride and prejudice the blow was struck and for a time the flash seemed imminent. For a long time a brave and rugged citizen of the little town, a man having the courage of his convictions and deeply trusted by his fellow-men, had been outspoken in his denunciation of the war. Wherever he was, he did not fear to express his belief in its illegality and unrighteousness. He was a strong man and an earnest one, and in his strength and earnestness lay his power over his fellow-men. He had represented them in Congress and he had done well. They believed in him, and now when he dared to say of the nation struggling for its very life that it was wrong, he found many followers, though some, like Bradford Waters, had already fallen from Vallandigham's side. For a while, he went his way unmolested, until one speech, a thought too bold in expression, brought down upon him the wrath—a wrath rather restraining than vindictive—of the government.

It was near midnight when a small company of soldiers from Cincinnati went to the door of Vallandigham's Dorbury home. The inmates of the house were abed, and all was darkness and silence. There was no reply to the thunderous summons on the panels, some inkling of the object of this midnight visit having leaked out or been suspected. The summons was repeated and while the men talked in low whispers below, a head was put out of an upstairs window and a voice called aloud some apparently meaningless words, which, however, were construed into a signal for aid. From this time, the soldiers delayed no longer, for in the present state of feeling the approach of reënforcements to those within would possibly result in bloodshed. This they were anxious to avoid, so making their way into the house they went from room to room, frequently having to break open locked and barred doors until they found the object of their search, and in spite of threat and protest, hurried away with him to a waiting train.

A small crowd collected, and followed the soldiers to the station, but with the exception of a stone occasionally hurled, it confined itself to threats and abuse.

" This will be heard from," said one.

" It will do more to make Ohio fight against the war than anything else."

" Kidnappers! kidnappers!" was the cry.

On the morrow the excitement in Dorbury was intense, but history has dealt sufficiently with all that was done then, with the speeches that were made, the bombastic letters that were written—the damage that was inflicted upon private property.

The town, iron-clad in its personal pride, gave itself up to an orgy of disloyalty. A tempest in a teapot, some one will say. But the spirit that raged in the teapot showed the temper of the larger cauldron which seethed over the same fire.

" What do you think of this later bit of work?" asked Davies on the way to the office the morning after the arrest.

"I think what I have always thought, that whatever is good for the Union is right." But his tone was not so assured as usual.

"You used to think a great deal of Vallandigham, though."

"In such a time as this, I have no time for personal feelings. I have said that before."

"Yes, it seems about true, we all seem to have taken leave of our senses and to have suspended the operations both of our country's constitution and of our natural affections."

"It is a strange time and we must change with the times."

"It is a horrible, a fanatical time, and I shall thank God when it is over, however the end may come, through Union or peaceful separation."

"I would rather see the country drenched in blood than the latter."

"Waters," said Davies slowly, as if the light were just dawning upon him, "I'm afraid you're a fanatic, I'm afraid you're a fanatic."

But Waters went on moodily and did not reply.

CHAPTER XVI

DOLLY AND WALTER

Down there in Virginia, where Walter had now settled into staying with a certain self-satisfaction, the tides of war flowed with vigor but did not reach and submerge the house where he kept the even tenor of his days. There were, of course, midnight visits at times from the soldiers of both sides. But the place enjoyed a peculiar exemption from molestation by either Confederate or Unionist. To the one, it was the home of old Colonel Stewart, an ardent Southerner. To the others, it was the place of abode of a paroled Union prisoner. Walter's position was anomalous, and although he was forced into it, he felt keenly that he was playing a double rôle. He no longer yearned to be with the Northern forces, but would it not be foolish to proclaim his defection from the house tops? The Southern soldiers and his neighbors looked upon him as a Unionist chafing at restraint, and they laughed at him for a caged bantam. Had their surmises been true, he would have scorned their laughter, but as it was, it cut him like a whip, because to his shame, what they laughed at, did not exist. Nor could he tell them this. They would have thought even less of him as a renegade who changed his allegiance and views under the stress of imprisonment.

Now and then, rather too frequently than he cared to own, he felt a thrill of envy for Nelson Etheridge, who had flung himself body and soul into the Union cause, and from whom he heard occasionally when he rode over to see Miss Etheridge, or when she and his sister Emily exchanged visits. " Here's a man for you," he would say to himself. " One who has not only dared, but continues to dare, one who, placed as I am placed, would feel the galling bonds of his restraint and do something besides feel ridiculously comfortable."

Perhaps it was because he was so young—and youth takes itself seriously, being in its own eyes either God or devil, hero or craven—that Walter was so hard upon his own failings. Sometimes, however, the truth that his position was not of his own seeking, forced itself upon his mind. But unwilling to accept this excuse, he questioned himself if he were not glad that things had turned out as they had. To this he must answer yes, and so he fell again to cursing his own complacency.

It is not to be supposed, however, that he lived constantly in a state of self-condemnation. Other moods were frequent and lasting. It took him a very short time to fall into the ways of a gentleman farmer, and he took a boyish pleasure in directing the work of the negroes about the place. His moments of greatest happiness were when he was riding about the fields on some duty or other, and he would be joined by Emily or Miss Etheridge. But his greatest moments of depression would follow when he saw, or thought he saw, a question or a reproach in the girl's eyes.

Since his arrival at his father's house, he had come to see more and more of this radiant Southern beauty, and a frank friendship had grown up between them. Friendship, he called it, for cherishing in his heart the memory of his regard for Nannie, he did not dream that love could touch him. But slowly and reluctantly, he began to compare the image in his heart with the fair girl at his side and the image suffered. Finally, he began to say that Nannie had appealed strongly to his boyish fancy, while this woman reached his maturer manhood. In spite of his self-questionings, Walter failed to see the humor implied in the fact that without any great moral, mental or spiritual cataclysm, this maturer manhood had come to him in a very short time after he had looked into Dolly's grey eyes.

She often rallied him about their first romantic meeting, and she would laugh the most musical of laughs as he told her about his trepidation as he approached the house. When she forgot herself, and was merry among friends, she had the habit of falling into the soft-Southern manner of speech.

"It's right down mean," she said to Walter in one of her bantering moods, "that you didn't let a body know you were coming. I reckon you and my brother Nelson would have had a mighty nice time together, but you were entirely too startling."

"If I had known that I was going to find friends behind those doors," he bent his gaze tenderly upon her, "I should have acted differently, knocked easily, or roared me as gently as a sucking dove."

"Poor Nelson, I don't reckon many folks would have stayed on and dared capture like he did; but Nelson always was such a daring boy."

Walter winced. He thought he saw the question in her eyes, and something veiled in what she said.

Did she despise him after all, and only give him the semblance of friendship for his sister's sake? The thought made him miserable, although he never stopped to tell himself what logical reason there was for his being miserable, if the girl whom he had known but a few weeks did despise him.

"The Union has gained a gallant man in your brother," he said, because his head was in a tumult, and he could not say anything else. She did not recognize the commonplaceness of his remark, however. It was praise for her brother, and so, sublime.

"Oh, I wish you could have known him," she went on. "You'd have been sure to love him. Don't you know," she said, with a sudden impulse, "since I've known you, I've always thought of you and him in the same company, marching and fighting together. I don't care in what uniform, blue or grey. There, there, now," she added, gravely, "I've made you feel bad, but don't let's think of it. Yours is the fortune of war, just as whatever happens to him will be."

Walter was pale from forehead to lips and it was the knowledge of this that checked the girl with the belief that she had pained him by touching the subject of his detention.

"I'm afraid you're not a very good Unionist," said the young man somewhat recovering himself.

"I'm a woman, Mr. Stewart, and I reckon you're too young to know just what that implies. I'm in favor of the Union, because Nelson's fighting for it, and he wouldn't do anything that he didn't think was right. But I am a southern girl, and I love the South. Now what am I going to do? You don't know, though, for it's only women who let their affections run against principle."

He gave her a quick, suspicious glance. She was unconscious. He was on the rack.

"It isn't only women," he said.

"You only say that to be polite, and because it's so different with you, but I know better."

He rose quickly and on the plea of some obligation moved away, leaving her to Emily's company and conversation.

The rest of the day was a trying time for Walter. It was now unmistakable. Dolly Etheridge had seen through him, had seen his weakness and his defection, and in her contempt for him delighted to stab him with her quiet sarcasm. What a thing he must be to call forth the girl's disgust. How she must look down upon him when she compared him with her brother, such a brother; and in fancy, he saw Nelson Etheridge sweeping the enemy before him to the huzzas of a great nation. Well, anyway, Dolly could not think less of him than he thought of himself.

He would rather not have seen her any more that night. But he had promised to go with Emily to take her home. He appeared at supper with the best grace possible, and when it was over, joined the girls for the ride in the moonlight. It would have been pleasant to him, this cantering by Dolly's side, with the moon, a silver globe above them, and the scent of magnolias coming sweetly to their senses, but that his mind was sadly busy with what she must be thinking of him. He kept a moody silence while the girls chattered on. Sometimes, even, in his desperation, he thought of violating his parole, but his face grew hot with shame, and the thought went as quickly as it came.

Dolly and Emily, because they both believed Walter immersed in sad thoughts, respected his silence, and when he had helped the girl alight at her door, and given the horse to a black servant aroused from somewhere, the former gave him her hand with a little sympathetic pressure that made his heart leap. But then, the next moment he was saying, "Bah, she is only sorry for having stabbed me so cruelly, but the reason for the stabbing remains."

As they turned their horses homeward again, Walter seemed in no better mood for talking than before. But the moonlight and the sweetness of the soft night seemed to have got into his sister's tongue. She drew her horse close to her brother's and laid her hand gently on his.

"I'm afraid you're not well, to-night, Walter. What's the matter?"

"Oh, nothing, nothing. I'm really very well."

"But you have been so silent, and I really believe Dolly expected you to talk to her."

"I hardly think she could have cared much, either one way or the other," he said bitterly.

"If you can say that, you know very little about Dolly, or in fact, about women at all. You must know that she likes you, and likes you very well."

"I don't believe it," said Walter doggedly, but something he did just at the moment to the horse he was riding, made her arch her neck and step out as daintily as a lady.

"But she does like you, and if she didn't, you would soon know it. She's very peculiar and as open as the day. She can never conceal her thoughts and feelings. Some people call it a fault, but I call it a virtue."

"One would think at times that she was sarcastic or spoke under a veil." He was making a great effort to be indifferent, but the bridle in his hand grew tense.

"Why, she's as innocent of such things as a child. How stupid you are, Walter. I never knew you to be so before, and I did so hope you would be good friends."

"Well, well, haven't we been?"

"It seemed so for awhile, but you were so different to-night."

"Was I? Did she notice it?" The question was eager.

"Being a woman, she could scarcely help noticing it."

"Well, I was thinking," he said lamely, and then burst out, "What a glorious night it is, and how sweet those magnolias are. I didn't notice it before. Why, Emily, it's good to be alive."

"One wouldn't have thought it of you a little while ago, you were so quiet and subdued."

"Oh, well, there are times when the beauty of a night sinks into our souls too deep for words." Walter winced in spirit at his own hypocrisy.

"There, I told Dolly that you felt more than you said."

"You told her that? She talks about me to you?"

"Oh sometimes you come up in the course of conversation."

"What a wonderful girl she is."

"You—do you think so?"

"That is, she shows a deep affection for her brother, which is commendable."

"Oh,—but—don't most sisters?"

"There are very few such sisters as I imagine Miss Etheridge and know you to be."

She forgave him instantly. "You dear old Walter."

"And you think she likes me?" It was sweet to him to say it after his bitter thoughts.

"I know she does, and you should have known it too."

"Her brother must be a fine fellow."

"You would like him, I know."

"Let's sit out and talk awhile. It's altogether too lovely to go in," said the young man, as they turned in at the gate.

"I shall like it," said Emily, and giving their horses to a groom, they sat down on the veranda steps. For a few moments there was a silence between them, and both sat gazing at the starry heavens. Then Walter said falteringly,

"I—I—really—I am very much interested in Miss Etheridge's brother. Tell me more about him."

Then his sister laughed, not teasingly nor banteringly, as some sisters would have done, but with a little satisfied note, and she said, "Brother mine, there is only one thing more transparent than glass," and her brother caught her about the waist, and kissed her for some reason not quite clear to himself. So they sat together long that night and talked of the Etheridges, brother and sister.

In the young man, his fellow-soldier, Walter evinced a polite and conservative interest, but he was apt to bring the conversation back to the sister when it seemed to have a tendency to remain too long away from her. If he found no more pertinent remark to make, he would turn to Emily and say, "So you think she likes me?" and this was sufficient to start the stream of talk flowing in the proper channel.

When, finally, they sought their rooms that night, and the young man dropped asleep, there was a smile on his lips, and the words on his tongue, "She likes me, she likes me."

CHAPTER XVII

WHEN LOVE STANDS GUARD

WHAT surprised Walter when the morning brought with waking a review of the night's happenings, was that Emily, simple Emily, who had never had a love affair in her life that he knew, should have discovered to him his own secret. Or maybe she had discovered nothing that really existed at the time. Perhaps the train had been laid, the fuse set, and her remark only been the match to set the whole agoing. However, it made no matter at all how or when it happened. It was true. Now to let Dolly know. It was remarkable how soon and how easily all his fears and misgivings had disappeared. It was as if this state of exultation had been waiting for him and he had but to step into it. Why had he delayed so long?

The days that followed were filled with softer sounds than the sounds of war, and doings that had no shadow or show of the harshness of the camp. Walter, dazzled by the glory of the new world that had opened up before him, forgot the hardness of his lot, forgot, perhaps, even the deeper sympathy that should have gone from him to the men in the field—for love is a jealous mistress. He walked and rode much with his sweetheart, by the grass-grown bridle paths and under the ancient trees. His heart sang a song to hers, and hers replied in kind. Emily, like a good sister, knew when to be judiciously absent, and Dolly understood all that he would say to her long before he dared speak.

It was not until the warm southern November was painting the hills and valleys that he told her of his love and his hope.

" It seems, somehow, Dolly, that I have no right to speak to you, placed as I am, but what am I to do ? The message beats at my heart until at times I think you must hear it. I love you and have loved you from the very first night that we met."

" Are you sure ? " she asked quietly, but with just a suspicion of mirth.

" I was never surer of anything in my life."

" Did you always know that you loved me ? "

" I did not always say it to myself as I say it now, sometimes tremblingly, sometimes with exultation, but I must always have known it, else why should your lightest word have had the power of making me happy or miserable ? "

They were walking slowly over the crisp pine

needles in the copse not far from the house. She drew closer to his side, and her hand slipped into his.

"Poor Walter," she said, "I used to make you miserable. I never wanted to do that because ——"

"Because?" he said eagerly.

"Because I do love you."

He took her in his arms and held her close to him. His head bowed humbly.

"What am I to be worthy of this?" he said at last.

"You are Walter, my Walter, my hero."

Even in that moment of ecstasy he winced at the word hero. He was not of the material of which heroes are made and he knew it. But he would not shadow their happiness now. Let her think well of him if she could. Later, he would try to deserve her, and after all, what man is so good, so upright as the woman who loves him believes?

Later, when the deep solemnity of the first betrothal had given way to a gayer mood, she asked him, "What will my Virginia friends say to my marrying a Yankee?"

"What can they say when you are more than half Yankee yourself?"

"I declare I'm not. I'm Southern clear through."

He took her hands and laughed down into her eyes. "No, you're not. You're just—just a woman, and I'm only a man and we're both more lovers than anything else, so let your friends say what they will," and the answer seemed to satisfy her. Walter, himself, was very well satisfied, and when two young people are perfectly satisfied with themselves and each other, the world is shut from their vision, and time trips a merry pace.

"Let us keep our sweet secret for awhile," she said when the lengthening shadows warned them that it was time even for a lover's tête-à-tête to be done.

"Let us," he assented, "if we can. It seems so much more our own, but, can we?"

"Oh, I can, I know, and you can of course, for it's only women who are untrustworthy with secrets."

"Yes, that's true, but there are secrets and secrets. There never was such a one as this before, so we have no foundation upon which to make a conclusion."

"You are a goose," she said, and then paid him for being one. Walter was right though. They went into supper and had not been at table five minutes before every one knew. Something in their faces or manner or the way they played with the food, laughed inconsequently, **cast** glances at each other, told more plainly than words what had happened. Love had put on them his subtle sign.

Of course, Walter being a man, thought that he was carrying off his part with wonderful grace and shrewdness. But when Emily teased Dolly as they were passing out on the veranda, the newly betrothed hid her blushing face and cried, "Oh, Emily, how did you know?"

It was within a few days after this that reports began to come to the residents in and about Fairfax of the presence of guerillas, foraging and marauding bands in the neighborhood and frequently greatly exaggerated accounts were given of their depredations. Walter heard them all with a sinking at the heart for the safety of his betrothed. She was alone there with only three or four black servants in whose valor or faithfulness he had little or no belief. The first night or two that the rumors were current, he contented himself with getting to horse, and in silence and secrecy patroling the road in front of the Etheridge cottage. Nothing occurred, but as the rumors grew darker, his state of mind became more perturbed and he decided upon more vigorous measures. But Dolly's danger had not occurred to him alone, and before he could break the subject to his sister, she had come to him with a troubled face.

"Walter," she said, "won't you excuse me—I —haven't been spying on you, but I've guessed where you've been the last two nights."

A thrill half of shame and half of pride in himself shook him.

"Well, wasn't I right, Emily?" he asked.

"Of course, you were, for the time being; but do you think it is enough? You know we had word from Miss Mason that the guerillas visited her place last night and if it hadn't been for the servants they would have been rude or worse. Now Dolly is poor and has so few negroes about her."

"Well, what can we do?"

"I wouldn't trust those black folks anyhow, since they've got notions of freedom in their heads."

"Nor I, but I can't go over there and stay."

"Dolly could come here."

"Would she? Do you think she would?"

"Of course she would. Mother and I both agree that this is altogether the best plan, and we wondered if you'd mind riding over for her to-night."

"Would I mind?"

The tone was quite sufficient, and nothing more was needed to be said.

The moon was at the full, and flooded the landscape with silvery light when accompanied by Sam, a slave boy to whom he had become greatly attached, and bearing the invitation from his mother and sister, Walter set out for Dolly's house. For a time they went their way in silence, and then Sam, with the uncontrollable desire of his race for lyric expression broke into a song that woke the echoes. The young man, he was hardly yet a master, even in his thoughts, listened with pleasure, until he saw a dark form beside the road rise up, gaze at them for a moment, and then disappear into the surrounding wood.

"Sh," said Walter, without mentioning what he had seen, "I don't believe I'd sing any more, Sam. There's no telling what we might start up."

"Wisht to de Lawd it 'ud be a 'possum," said Sam, chuckling with easy familiarity, but he hushed his song.

"If we started up anything, it might not be something so pleasant for you as a 'possum."

"Not pleasant fu' me," replied Sam, "huh uh, you do' know dis hoss."

"So you'd leave me, would you, you rascal? Well, you're a great one."

"'Spec's I'd have to leave you ef I couldn't tek you erlong."

As they approached their destination, Walter suddenly drew rein and laid his hand on his

companion's bridle. He pointed quickly and silently to the form of a man clearly outlined in
the moonlight. He was standing at the front of
the cottage window attempting to peer into the
room through a crack between the lower blind
and the sill. So intent was he upon his spying
that he had not noticed the approach of the
others.

"Dismount here," said Walter, "and tie the
horses under the shadow of that mulberry tree.
I believe there's mischief going on."

The negro did as he was bidden and hastened
back to his companion's side, just as the intruder
walked up and began knocking at the door.
After some delay, the voice of a negro from
within, questioned, "Who's dat?"

"Never mind," was the answer, "you open
up."

The silent watcher was breathless with interest, but he kept cool enough to say, "Sam, you
slip around to the cabins, and rouse what
negroes you can. Be ready for whatever
happens, for there's no telling how many of
them there are." Without a thought of his
joke about desertion, Sam slipped away, leap-
ing across the moonlit places from shadow to
shadow while Walter crept nearer to the man at
the door.

It had not been opened, but a negro came

from a side entrance and confronted the intruder.

"Why don't you open the door?" was the harsh question fired at the dark Cerberus.

"Well, suh, I didn't jes' know who you was, an' I t'ought mebbe I could tell you whutevah you wanted to know."

"It's none of your damn business who I am. I'm here in the name of the law, and you'd better open up all-fired quick or it'll be the worse for you."

The negro went back around the house and in a few minutes the door opened. As he passed the light, Walter saw that he wore the uniform of a Confederate officer.

The door closed behind him, but Stewart becoming spy in turn, came near enough to hear what was said within.

"Where is your mistress?" in the officer's voice.

"She done retahed, suh."

"Tell her I wish to see her."

"She done retahed."

"Very well, let her get up. Tell her that her brother is supposed to be skulking within the lines, and that I am sent to search the house for him."

"You kin such de house."

"I shall begin with her room."

" Dey is no one in huh room, but huh, suh."

" How dare you talk back to me, you black hound ? "

The harsh voice was suddenly checked, and then Walter heard another that made his heart leap within his throat.

" Never mind, Mingo," it said, " I am out of my room now. Lieutenant Forsythe," went on Dolly calmly, " you are at liberty to begin there now, and search where you please." The tone reeked with scorn.

" You will go with me," was the reply.

" A trusted servant may accompany you."

" You will go with me, I said."

" As you will, lieutenant, but this is the way you pay your scores—come when there is no man in the house save a servant, to take revenge for a woman's no."

" We will not discuss that matter now, Miss Etheridge."

Walter had pushed the door open and he saw that the man's face went red and white at Dolly's words. He saw too, the fierce eyes of the black servant fixed on Forsythe, and for one instant, he wondered if he were needed. In the next, he had flung the door open and stepped into the room. Every eye turned upon him, and he said clearly, " And why, Lieutenant Forsythe, must the lady go with you ? "

"Oh, Walter," Dolly cried, and then checked herself with a sigh of relief. The lieutenant was livid.

"And who in hell are you?" he asked in a tense voice.

"I am Walter Stewart, at your service, lieutenant."

"The paroled Yankee, eh? Oh, I see," he said in a tone that put murder in Walter's heart. "It is thus that you are protected, Miss Etheridge?"

"You may go on with your search, lieutenant, that you have a perfect right to do, but Miss Etheridge, protected or not, will not leave this room."

The two men stood glaring into each other's faces, while Mingo, relaxed from his vigilance, was chuckling in a corner. On a sudden, there was a rush of feet without, and four brawny men sprang into the room. The open door and the loud voices had attracted Forsythe's minions, who had been placed at a convenient distance. The lieutenant smiled grimly as his men surrounded Walter.

"I reckon, Mr. Stewart," he said with a sneer, "that you'll go a bit slower now."

"I'm not so sure of that, lieutenant," said Walter, and as he spoke, four negroes, led by Sam, and bearing stout clubs swept into the room.   The soldiers, if such the ragged guerillas, whom Forsythe had taken as his accomplices could be called, were completely taken by surprise, and wilted as the threatening blacks, now man to man lined up beside them.

While the disappointed officer stood there chewing his mustache with rage, Walter had time for a few reflections upon the fidelity of a people whom he so little trusted because their fidelity militated against themselves, and it settled something in his mind that made his eyes flash and his lips press close together.

"You may proceed with your search now, lieutenant," said Dolly sweetly.

"It is unnecessary now. I suppose our bird has flown, and I shall not put myself to the trouble of searching your empty rooms."

"Are you sure that you did not know before you came, lieutenant, that you would not find my brother here?"

"I am sure that I have found out some things that I did not know before," he answered, glancing meaningly at the girl's protector. And then, the devil, which is in every man, became strong in Walter. It overcame him. His fist shot out, and Lieutenant Forsythe's lips spilled blood. The officer's eyes grew green and his hand went quickly to his holster, and then, the veneering that had cracked and shown the brute in him, closed again, and wiping the blood from his mouth, he said with the calmness of intense anger, "What this calls for, Mr. Stewart, is entirely beyond the limits of my present official duty. Will you grant me the pleasure of a few minutes' private conversation?" They stepped outside and a brief whispered conversation ensued. They were equally placid when they returned.

"Attention! about face! forward, march!" and without further word or sign, Forsythe and his minions marched away.

"Follow them quietly, Sam, and see that they are up to no mischief, and you, Miss Etheridge, get your things on, for you must go with me." He had forgotten all about the formal invitation.

"When is it to be?" she asked in reply.

He would have tried to evade, but she looked at him so steadfastly and earnestly that he could not.

"To-morrow morning," he said simply, "but it is to be taken up as a merely personal matter, so I beg that you say nothing about it. Now go."

She pressed his hand quickly.

"Come 'long, Miss Dolly," said Mingo, still chuckling with glee, "hyeah 'Mandy stan'in' behime de do' wid a flatiron. I reckon ef Mas' Stewa't hadn' 'a' come, she'd a' to' dat game roostah up 'fo' I could a' said Jack Robinson."

When Sam had returned and reported all well, they got to saddle and started on their way, two of the negroes mounting and coming behind to prevent treachery. Dolly and Walter rode side by side, and Sam, who rode before, had neither eyes nor ears.

"Do you really believe he was looking for Nelson?" she asked.

"Do you?"

"Oh, Walter, he has a grudge, and he is relentless. He proposed to me once, and he has pursued me ever since."

"For that reason, if no other, I shall try to kill him to-morrow," and the shadow being convenient, he kissed her.

There was some commotion in the house when the party reached home, and the story was told in its entirety. But nothing save praise fell to Walter's lot for his action. Dolly respected his wishes and said nothing of the impending duel, though her heart ached for her lover.

"I shall see you before you go in the morning," she said when they were alone for a moment before parting that night.

"I shall be leaving very early, before you are up."

"Before I am up! Walter, what can you be thinking of me? Why, I shall not go to bed."

"You must, dear, for I shall, and I shall sleep well."

"As you say, but I shall see you in the morning, nevertheless."

Walter called Sam to him as he went up to his room.

CHAPTER XVIII

AN AFFAIR OF HONOR

THE arrangements for the meeting between Walter Stewart and Lieutenant Forsythe were as simple as the brevity of their conversation indicated. The whole matter was to be kept a profound secret as much on account of Walter's position as a paroled prisoner as because of the other's place in the army. They were to face each other in a small open space under the trees that lined a little creek about three miles from the Etheridge cottage. They were both familiar with the place and agreed upon it with equal readiness. Because of the secrecy which they wished maintained, there were to be no witnesses beside the two seconds, but each might bring with him a trusted friend or servant. Thus promptly, they arranged the affair leaving only to the assistants yet to be chosen the task of marking the ground and giving the signal. Pistols were the weapons.

When, after parting with Dolly, Walter called Sam to his room, it was to dispatch him on a delicate and doubtful errand. Recognizing the peculiar attitude of his neighbors towards him, he had formed but few friendships and these only of the most tentative kind. Now, in this emergency, he needed a friend and a confidant. His mind turned to but one person, a young Dr. Daniel, whose frank manner had won him as much as he dared yield himself. He now sent the servant to bring to him this man upon the plea of most pressing business.

In less than an hour, the young physician was with him. He was an open-faced, breezy looking young man of nine-and-twenty, or thereabouts, with the assured manner of perfect self-possession and self-reliance.

He came into the room with a soft though brisk step, but stopped in surprise to see Walter pacing up and down the room.

"Come in, doctor."

"Why, why, man, from the expression of that rascal of yours, I expected to find you in bed tossing with a raging fever or laid up with a broken leg."

"I shall not be your patient, to-night, doctor, to-morrow, who can say?"

"Eh, what's this? Not thinking of suicide, are you?"

"I'm thinking of how good a shot my opponent may be. The fact is, Dr. Daniel, I called you here on a business that is almost, if not wholly impertinent. But I hope you will pardon and help me, for there is no one else to whom I may turn." He then recounted to him the events of the night; the physician's face, already inclined to ruddiness, growing redder and angrier as he went on.

"Now, doctor," concluded Walter, "I am sure that Forsythe's intentions were neither honest nor official, and I have only tried to do my duty. Is it too much to ask you to forget what I am politically, and to be my friend and second in this matter?"

"Forget what you are? Damn what you are, Stewart. I'll tell you what I'll do, man, I'll change places with you. I'll let you be my second."

"It's my fight."

"But don't you see it's a nasty business, and might get you into complications."

"I am willing to risk all that."

"Oh, come now, be sensible. The lady's brother is a good friend of mine."

"The lady is a good friend of mine."

"But I know the whole story; how he has tried to annoy that girl ever since she rejected him two years ago as any girl of decency and spirit would have done. I know he has always kept just outside the limit that would give her brother the right to fill his carcass full of lead. He has overstepped it now, and I want a chance to get a shot at the dirtiest hound in all Virginia. Give it to me."

"Wish I could, old man, but I want it myself."

"Oh, well, I always was a selfish dog. It's your say and if you won't, you won't; but anyhow, I'm with you, and I'll be in at the death if I can't have the brush."

"Thank you, doctor, your kindness is even greater than I could have hoped for, even from you."

"Yours isn't, or you'd have given me a shot at that cur; but remember if he happens to hit you, and God forbid that, I get the next chance at his hide."

"I wouldn't want to leave the business to a better man, and now, let us complete our arrangements, and then you may get to bed."

They talked for a short time longer, and then Walter conducted the physician to his room, while he gave his attention to one or two other duties. The last words the buoyant young Southerner said to him as he began to undress were, "Um, you're a lucky dog—a shot at Forsythe!"

It was before the darkness of the night had given way to the morning's grey that the men

were up and ready for the saddle. Dr. Daniel
had already reached the lawn where Sam was
holding the horses. Walter loitered down the
hallway, half expecting, yet half doubting that
he should see Dolly.

"She's asleep, of course," he told himself, "and
I'm glad of it. How could I expect her to get up
after such a night as she has had. I was a brute
to think of it." Nevertheless, there was a dissatisfied feeling tugging at his heart as he
stepped out on the veranda. But his foot had
scarcely touched the floor when his eye caught
the flash of a woman's white shawl up under
some vines that overhung the porch. His heart,
suddenly relieved from its tension, gave a great
leap as he hastened towards her.

"Dolly," he said, "I was afraid you wouldn't
come. Indeed, I didn't want you to, dear."

"I had to come, if only to bid you Godspeed,
Walter. Come back to me, you will, won't
you?"

"To answer that, lies beyond me, my darling,
but I will try. If I don't ——"

"Don't say that—you will."

"Good-bye, now."

"Good-bye, Walter, good-bye, and strength to
you and a safe return. Good-bye."

She went back and he hastened down and
swung into the saddle.

"We must not keep the gentlemen waiting," he said to the doctor as they rode away slowly until out of ear-shot of the house.

"It will be enough to leave him lie waiting afterwards, and I hope you will leave him for a long wait, after it's all over."

"Well, it's a chance, you know, and I'm willing to take it; if he leaves me, instead, I guess Sam here, can take me home across his horse."

Sam was trailing along, carrying the pistol case, but he caught the words, and spurred up to his master.

"Mas' Waltah," he said solemnly, " ef dat man hits you, dey kin bu'n me er hang me, but he ain' gwine leave dis place alive."

The doctor suddenly halted horse and turned on the negro.

"Now look here, Sam," he said, "it's all right for you to be protecting your master, but whatever happens, if you raise a hand against John Forsythe, I'll kill you on the instant. When your master is done with him, he's my meat, and he'll hardly take the reckoning of us both."

Sam looked appealingly to his master.

"That's right," the latter replied, " you're not in this part of it, Sam, but you did your share last night. Anyhow, I'm not counting on leaving work for anybody this morning."

For the rest of the journey, they rode in silence,

but Walter's thoughts were busy with the events that had filled his life in the weeks since he had left Ohio. He reviewed the change that had come to him in his feelings towards the cause he had espoused. He saw how remorse for the disagreement with his father, his affection for his family and the glamour of the South had all combined to win him from a righteous allegiance, and made him lukewarm or indifferent to what he had once felt to be the absolute right. He saw that in spirit, if not in deed, he was as much a deserter as the veriest renegade, who stole from the marching ranks to hide in the thickets and by ways until his comrades had passed on. He saw how much weaker a man he was now than on the day when he had gone out from his father's house in Dorbury, though he did not see that the weakening process had been excusable, even inevitable. Though he held himself mercilessly up to his own criticism, the very fact that he was able to see these things in himself clearly, was evidence of the approach of a new state of mind, a change subtler than either of the others had been. He had begun to get back to himself, to be a man stronger than his surroundings, with a spirit independent of his affections.

At first contact with it, to him, as to many others beyond his years, the condition of the South, its life and its people, had seemed all chivalry and romance. The events of the past and the present day's business, had done more to tear aside this veil than anything else could have done. It was clear to him now that they were not all gods and goddesses in Dixie—that if it were an Eden, at least it was not free from serpents. He had received a royally good shaking up, and now he began to perceive that some hasty conclusions which he had reached were not based upon fact. One of these was that the North was eaten up by commercialism while the South was free from it; another that Northern honor and Southern honor were two essentially different things; both these beliefs died an early death as he reflected that here too, men bought and bartered, sold and intrigued. The occurrences which had taken place within the last few months under his eyes now reacted one upon the other with the result of placing him surely, strongly and logically where his first enthusiasm had placed him, and for the first time since he had been paroled, the irksome hatefulness of his situation was borne in upon him. Now he chafed to be in the field again. Now he felt the thrill of fighting for a great cause. His eyes were flashing and his teeth clenched hard when the voice of the doctor called him to the business at hand.

"Here we are," he cried as gaily as though

they were a party reaching the picnic grounds, "and we're the first here, of course."

They dismounted and tied their horses, and then began examining the ground. It was a plot of greensward, well surrounded by trees, and sloping with a slow incline to a little creek that ran gurgling past—a quiet, pretty enough place, but its very seclusion had made it the recipient of many a bloody secret in those days when men settled affairs of honor according to the code. Two trees stood opposite each other about twenty paces apart, and these had won the name of the "duelling trees," because the distance between them being paced, the principals were usually placed, one under each, and many a deadly combat had been waged beneath their softly sighing branches.

The grey dawn had given way to the warmer hues of morning when two other riders cantered into the circle of trees and halted.

"It's Forsythe," said the doctor.

"And he only brings one of his troopers with him as second."

"If it is true that he went on that errand last night without authority, it is just as well that he does not have too many in his secret," was the rejoinder.

The men greeted each other with the utmost formality, though there was a touch of brusque-

ness in the physician's recognition of the lieutenant.   While the two principals walked apart,
their seconds paused for a brief conference as to
conditions.   In a little while, Dr. Daniel came
to Walter.

"Are you ready and steady, old man?"

"Both," was the calm reply.

"The conditions are these; you are to be stationed at twenty paces, back to back.   At the
word, you are to turn and fire where you stand,
then each has the privilege of advancing, firing
until one or the other is hit.   Are you satisfied?"

"Perfectly."

"Very well, we are ready," said the doctor to
Forsythe's trooper, and together they paced off
the ground, already so well known.   Then the
men were put in their places, and each second
saw to the condition of his principal's weapon.
Dr. Daniel stationed himself to the left, and
midway the ground, while the trooper took a
like position to the right.

"Are you ready, gentlemen?" said the latter.

"We are ready."

"One."

Then the clatter of horses' hoofs broke the
morning stillness, and he paused.   Both men
waited with manifest impatience, but neither
spoke.

"Go on," said the doctor.   "Quick!"

"Two."

Forsythe half turned, but it was too late. A squad of horsemen in grey uniform burst into the enclosure and rode between the men.

"Walter Stewart," said the sergeant, "I arrest you upon the charge of violating your parole."

"Can you not wait just one moment until this business can be dispatched," said Walter calmly.

But the officer spurred away from him with a curt, "Your business is not ours."

"Never mind, Forsythe," screamed Daniel, "I'll take the job off of Stewart's hands."

"Lieutenant Forsythe is also under arrest," said the sergeant.

Forsythe went very white, but stood calm as a statue.

"You took a miserable, cowardly way to save yourself," he said when he and Walter were brought together.

"You are mistaken, lieutenant," said the sergeant breaking in, "one of your own men was the informant."

The lieutenant bit his lip. The three prisoners, for the trooper was also put under arrest, mounted their horses and were surrounded by a close guard.

"Why am I too not arrested?" stormed the doctor.

"We had no orders regarding you, sir," was

the reply, and the little cavalcade cantered away, leaving the physician swearing with feeling and distinction.

"Never mind," he said at last. "Let's go home, Sam. If that old trooper had been a bit quicker, Virginia might have been rid of the meanest sneak that ever scourged her; but instead of that, the party is broken up and nobody gets out of the mess but the doctor and the darky, neither one worth arresting. Come, let's go home."

CHAPTER XIX

JUSTICE

AFTER the arrest of Walter, the doctor and Sam rode back over their tracks one as disconsolate as the other. It was not a pleasant duty that loomed up before them in the all too near future. Walter was gone. He would be missed and questions would be asked. Then what?

"Oh, Lord," sighed the doctor, "Sam, what are we going to do? What are we going to say to them when they ask for him?"

"Well, hit don' seem dey's nuffin else fu' me to do but to tell de trufe."

"My Lord, you *are* in desperate straits, that's always a man's last resort. Now, for my part, I'd a good deal rather lie if it would do any good. But the devil's going to be raised, and they'll be sure to find out. Biff! there goes my reputation. I tried to persuade your master to let me take this business on my hands. It would have been a good deal better to have faced Forsythe and have shot him or been shot than to face these bereaved women. But I'm in for it now, so come along, Sam. You take a hint from me. If I decide to tell the truth, you tell it. If I decide to lie, you fall in and outlie the devil and stick to it."

As they neared the Stewart home, the spirits of both of them sank lower still. The sun was now overhead, and was fast drying the dew-laden grass by the roadside. The day was clear and bright, or they might have taken for an apparition the white faced figure that stepped out in the road before them.

The doctor drew in his horse with an exclamation, and Sam's eyes threatened to leave their sockets.

"Where is he? Where is he?" cried Dolly. "What has happened to him?"

The dumbfounded men gazed first at the misery-distraught woman, and then, helplessly at each other.

"Oh, don't keep me in suspense. Tell me, where is Walter?" She had thrown aside all reserve and false modesty, and stood before them, self-confessed, a woman distressed for the safety of her lover.

"Why—why—Miss Etheridge," stammered Daniel.

"You tell me, Sam. I command you to tell me the truth. I see in Dr. Daniel's eyes his intention to hide something from me."

The slave looked at his companion for guid-
ance, but getting no help from him, he mum-
bled, "Mas' Walter, w'y, he went wid de lootenant."

"Went with him? What do you mean? Was
he hurt? Have you deserted him? Oh, doctor,
please, please tell me. It was for me that he
went into this."

Daniel dismounted, and throwing his bridle
over his arm, he began leading the girl towards
the house.

"I'll tell you the truth," he said, and as briefly
and gently as possible, he related what had taken
place.

She heard him through in silence, and then
asked, "What will they do with him?"

"That I cannot tell, Miss Etheridge, but I
don't see how they can do much when the truth
is known."

"But will the truth be known?"

"I cannot vouch for that, either, but whatever
I can do to make it known, shall be done. I am
going up home to arrange my affairs, so that I
may be away, and then I shall start for Colonel
Braxton's headquarters, whither he will be
taken."

"Will you take a letter for me?"

"With pleasure."

"Thank you, doctor, thank you for your kindness to him and to me. I will have the letter ready when you return. Good-bye until then."

She was hastening away, but he detained her. "I am going up to the house," he said.

"You must not, I will break it to them as you cannot."

"But do you think it quite right?" he asked with a look of relief that belied his anxious tone.

"I can do it better than you. So do not wait for me. Mount and lose no time." She hurried on, and he rejoined Sam.

"It's all right, Sam. Just keep your mouth shut. The telling will be done for us better than we can do it.

"By Jove," he said later, as he left the servant at the gate and rode on past. "If I could find a woman who loved me like that, I'll be hanged if I wouldn't risk it. I would."

With swift, but reluctant steps, Dolly made her way homeward and sought out Emily and her mother. Her face was pale and drawn with pain and her girl-companion saw at once that something was wrong.

"What is it, Dolly?" she asked hastening to her.

"Let me sit down, I don't know what you will say to me, Mrs. Stewart, and you, Emily, how you will feel towards me."

"Nothing can ever change us towards you, Dolly, so be calm," said Emily, putting her arms around her.

"I should have told you last night, but he wouldn't let me, he was afraid you would be worried."

"Is it about Walter?" exclaimed his mother. "What has happened to him?"

"He is at Colonel Braxton's headquarters, under arrest."

"Under arrest?" cried the two women.

"But Dolly;" said Emily, "how could they arrest him? He was paroled."

"Oh, you will think that I am a wicked, heartless girl, for it is all my fault."

"Your fault? How?" Emily's tone was colder, and she withdrew her arm from Dolly's waist.

"Don't leave me, Emily, till you understand. There was a personal encounter last night between Walter and Lieutenant Forsythe, and it resulted in a meeting between them this morning."

"A duel?"

"It would have been, but they were both arrested by a squad this morning and taken away."

"Why did you not tell us this before, Dolly, so that we might have stopped it?" said Mrs. Stewart sternly.

"Walter forbade me and I could not violate his confidence."

"There are times when even a violation of confidence might be justifiable."

The girl raised her tear-stained face to the older woman's. "You do not understand," she said. "He was involved on my account, and he trusted me. Suppose I had violated this trust, told you and the matter had been stopped by you? What would they have said? 'His mother intervened to save him.' Mrs. Stewart, Walter's honor is as dear to me as to you or Emily, and I could not do that."

"Forgive me, child, you are right, but this is very hard."

"I know it. But though I could not save him then without dishonor, I shall try to help him now, by writing the whole story to Colonel Braxton."

"Who will take it?"

"Dr. Daniel is going to the camp to intercede for Walter, and will call for my letter soon. I will go now and write it. Do try to be calm. They can't be hard upon him when they know what a hero he has been."

Mrs. Stewart patted the girl's hand gently and said, "His mother and sister will try to be as brave as ——"

"His sweetheart," cried Dolly, blushing, and

taking the grey-haired woman in her arms, she kissed her and sped from the room. Emily laughed.

"Why, daughter, how can you laugh at such a time?" asked her mother.

"Because I feel so sure that Walter is safe, and will come back to us unharmed and without dishonor."

"Don't be sanguine, dear. The conditions of war are very different from those of peace."

"I know, mother, but would you have had him do less?"

"I don't know, and, yes, I do; your father's son could have done no less."

It was not long before Dr. Daniel came hastening back, but quick as he was, Dolly Etheridge was ready with her letter.

"I want you to forgive me," he said, "for my part in this affair, but you must understand that I am not greatly to blame. I begged Stewart to let me chip in, but he's an awfully proud fellow, you see, and he wouldn't let me do it. I was particularly anxious to get a chance at Forsythe. But your son, Mrs. Stewart, said it was his quarrel, and I could only play second fiddle. To be sure, I might have locked him in his room and gone as proxy, but I didn't think he'd like it."

"Why that would have been horrible," exclaimed Emily.

"Yes, but you'd have had your brother with you now."

"We should not have wanted him at that cost," was the sister's reply.

"No, Walter has been perfectly right," added the mother.

"Perhaps I did the best thing, after all," said the doctor ruefully; "but it's pretty hard to see such a chance escape never to return."

"Had you any quarrel with Lieutenant Forsythe?"

"Oh, no, no special quarrel. It was just general principles with me. I really believe the Confederate army would have voted your son a medal if he had rid them of a hound who gained his position through the worst influence, and holds it through duplicity. But I mustn't stand here chattering all morning. I am quite ready to take your letter, Miss Dolly, and I am sure it will do as much good as you want it to do."

Miss Etheridge handed him her missive with a blush. "Bring him back with you," she said.

"Well, I won't promise to do just that, but if I don't, I'll bring you good news anyhow, and I won't spare any time in getting this into the proper hands. Good-morning to you, ladies, and good cheer," and the good doctor leaped into his saddle and cantered away, leaving behind him a cheerier household than he had found.

It was ten miles to his destination, but he made short work of it, sent his message through the lines and received safe conduct to the colonel. This officer was a grizzled veteran who had seen service in the Mexican war, and who was bent on doing for the raw material that he had in hand what years of service had done for him. He was as kind of heart as he was brusque of manner. To him, Dr. Daniel came with his own story and Dolly's letter, which the colonel read grimly.

"You are a friend of the prisoner's, I suppose?"

"Yes, I haven't known him long, but I have learned to like him right well."

"Do you know that this liking of yours and your connection with the affair is likely to involve you in difficulty?"

"Well, now, I hadn't thought of that, but it doesn't matter in the least."

The colonel bent industriously over the paper in his hand, and a smile flickered through his grey mustache.

"Are you acquainted also with Lieutenant Forsythe?"

Daniel straightened himself up angrily. "I know Forsythe."

"I said Lieutenant Forsythe."

"Beg pardon, colonel, but——"

"Enough, suh. Who is this Miss Etheridge?"

"She's a daughter of old Nelson Etheridge, of Rockford, sir."

"Who was related, I believe, to the Etheridges of Mecklenbu'g county?"

"Well, sir, I'm not just up on genealogy, and all that sort o' thing, but I dare say you're right. Most all Virginians are related, you know. It's become a state habit."

Again the colonel had recourse to the papers to hide his amusement. When he looked up again, he said,

"I shall have to detain you, Dr. Daniel, until I look further into this case. Discipline has been altogether too lax here of late, and while disaffection has not become common in Virginia, there is altogether too great a tendency towards it."

"I hope you don't feel any doubt about me, colonel?"

"It isn't a matter of personal feeling."

"Of course not, I ought to have known that. In fact, I did know it, and yet I feel that you are saying, 'What is an able-bodied fellow like that doing at home?' Well, I'm not home for choice or for all time. Yet there are some things to be done before I can go where the rest of the fellows of my age are. There are women and children to be looked after and dosed. Until now, there have been things outside of the army that

I could do for Virginia, but as soon as a breathing time comes, I shall be where I should be."

The colonel's eyes were very bright as he looked at the young man, but he only said, "No doubt," and called an officer to take Daniel away.

"There's a man who would make a good fighter, but a damned bad soldier," was the veteran's mental comment. "He's too free and easy."

"Bring in the prisoner, Stewart," was his command to the orderly.

The appearance of Walter was hardly that of a felon when he came into the presence of the commanding officer. His eyes were clear, his head high and his step firm. There was no sign of fear in the manner in which he met his judge's gaze.

"Your name is —— ?"

"Walter Stewart."

"And you were until first taken, a soldier of the Northern army?"

"I was."

"You were taken when within the Confederate lines, and were paroled when you might have been dealt with as a spy."

"My business within your lines was perfectly clear."

"That does not alter the case. You were paroled and violated the parole."

"I do not feel that the latter is the case, sir."

"What?" cried the colonel sternly. "Do you dare to deny it?"

"I deny none of the facts of the case, sir, I only question their construction."

"You have no right to question, suh, you are a prisoner to be judged. The case to my mind is perfectly clear against you."

"You are the judge," said Walter calmly.

"You were found, suh, in the very act of an encounter with a Confederate officer, after having assaulted him on the night before. We consider, suh, that you have violated your parole, and broken your word of honor."

"When Virginia thinks that by protecting a defenceless woman, a man tarnishes his honor or forfeits his word, I begin to feel sorry for my father's state."

"Suh, you are not the gyardian of Virginia's honah."

"I am the custodian of my own, though."

"Then you should have seen better to it than to have broken your parole. You know the consequences."

"I am not afraid of the consequences. I am willing to abide by them. But I do not think that I have violated my parole. I have not taken up arms against the Confederate states, unless they are warring against their own defenceless women. Nor have I given aid or comfort to your enemies, unless you consider as an enemy, a woman who has never by word or deed shown anything but allegiance to the South she loves."

" Ahem ! " said the colonel.

" Furthermore, my quarrel, my encounter, was not against your government, but against the injustice of one man. It was not an encounter involving national views, but a purely personal encounter."

" In troublous times like these, no encounter with an officer of ours can be considered as personal."

"I hope, sir, that you have not also suspended the rule in regard to respect for women."

" You are pleased to be impertinent, and yet I answuh that I hope Virginia will never be guilty of that." Walter bowed.

" I understand that you are a son of the late Colonel Stewart, a Virginia gentleman ? "

" I was never more his son than now."

"I doubt that. I knew your father."

" My father, placed in the same position I was, would, I believe, have acted as I did."

" Without doubt—I beg your pardon," the colonel checked himself. " But yours are rules of civil life, and your laws are for civilians; at present, we are under military rule."

"Having been a soldier, I understand that. I am in your hands."

"Sergeant of the guard, you will hold the prisoner under arrest until further orders. I will look into your case and consider it further. Retire. A moment, sergeant." The non-commissioned officer paused just out of ear-shot of Walter, and the colonel whispered, "Treat him well, sergeant, he's a Stewart cleah through."

After the dismissal of Walter, Lieutenant Forsythe was brought into the colonel's presence. The conference between him and his superior officer was short and decisive.

"Lieutenant Forsythe, you gave as your reason for entering the house of Miss Etheridge, that you were on a search for her brother."

"I did."

"You were not aware that her brother had been for some time in the Union army?"

"I had received reliable information that led me to believe that he had returned and was in hiding at home."

"After gaining entrance into the house, why did you insist upon Miss Etheridge's accompanying you in your search?"

Forsythe hesitated and turned color under the colonel's glance.

"I wished to be able to watch her face and so tell when I was upon the scent."

" Why, when you had the chance to search the house without her, did you not do it ? "

"I was sure her brother had been given time and opportunity to escape."

"Now, Lieutenant Forsythe, will you tell me by whose orders you went upon this search for Nelson Etheridge ? "

" I thought that the capture of an enemy —— "

" Will you answer my question ? "

" Upon no one's specific orders, but —— "

"No buts about it. I am answwuhed. Were you ever a suitor for Miss Etheridge's hand ? "

" I consider that a personal question, sir."

Forsythe saw that the hope for him was gone and he could be no worse off by taking a stand on dignified effrontery.

" Oh, you consider it a personal question ? "

"I do, and one that has nothing to do with my service."

"And as such, you refuse to answwuh it ? Very well. You have no doubt understood the rules of this command in regyard to the treatment of women ? "

" Yes—but —— "

" That will do, Lieutenant Forsythe. A court-martial will attend to your case."

The lieutenant saluted and was taken away under guard. Walter and Dr. Daniel were then summoned.

"Young man," said the colonel to the former, "I regret that I find cause neither to hold nor to punish you. I regret, too, that you have chosen a course alien to your father's traditions and beliefs. But that, of course, is not my affair. I advise you, in the future, however, to keep cleah of collisions with our officers, or the next time you may not get off so easily."

Walter felt it the part of wisdom to make no reply, and so merely bowed.

"You, Dr. Daniel," said the colonel, turning to the physician, "will always find a welcome here, and whenever, if ever, you choose to throw your lot in with us, I hope to have you in my command."

"Thank you, colonel, thank you, sir."

The two men were conducted safely away from camp and set on their homeward way.

"By Jove, Stewart," said the doctor heartily, "I wish you weren't a Yankee!"

"I'm hardly a Yankee, doctor, as you use the term. But knowing Ohio, and knowing Virginia through such men as you, I am more than ever for the Union that will keep two such states together, let that Union be bought at whatever price it may."

The two men clasped hands across their saddle bows. The physician took Walter's praise as ingenuously as a child.

"I wish," he said, "that more Northerners knew us Southerners."

"If the two sections did know each other better, a deal of blood might be saved."

It was a grave ride home, but the rejoicings at the end of the journey compensated for all the serious thought along the way.

"Bless you, Dr. Daniel," said Mrs. Stewart fervently.

"Oh, don't thank me, Mrs. Stewart. I'm not a drop in the bucket. It was Miss Dolly's letter that fixed everything."

"Dolly's letter!" cried Walter.

The girl blushed, and the doctor added, "Maybe I'm telling tales out of school."

"You shall tell me about it, Dolly," said Walter with glowing eyes. This was perhaps only an excuse to lead her away from the rest for a walk in the arbor. What excuse Dr. Daniel gave for leading Emily in an opposite direction matters not, but it must have been satisfactory, for Mrs. Stewart found the housewife's excuse of her work to leave them, and the doctor stayed to supper.

CHAPTER XX

THE VISION OF THE BLACK RIDER

DESPITE the apparent cheerfulness with which Mary Waters went her way in the Woods household, she was not entirely her own old self. There was an air about her not so much of sadness as of repression. She tried, as well as the circumstances of the household allowed, to be alone, although Nannie, feeling that brooding over her experiences must be unprofitable to her friend, attempted to correct this tendency in her. She was not always successful, for notwithstanding the pliancy of her disposition with those whom she loved, Bradford Waters' daughter had something of a will of her own, and there were times when she would elude Nannie's vigilance or repel her advances and wander away to indulge her moods to herself.

As the midsummer approached, she grew restless and preoccupied and often she would awake Nannie at night by starting up with cries of terror. But on being questioned, the only reply

she would make was that she had been dreaming.
Her dreams she would not tell at first.

Finally, the fancy so grew upon her that
Nannie began to tax her with keeping something
back. Mary continued reticent, but worn and
weak, she at last surrendered to her friend's
stronger nature.

"You've just got to tell me what it is, Mary
Waters," said Nannie. "Something is troubling
your mind, and you are troubling mine."

"But it's such a foolish thing, Nannie."

"I don't care. Folly is none the worse for
being shared with some one."

"Do you believe in dreams?"

"I don't know, tell me yours, and I'll see. If
I believe it means anything, I'll tell you, honestly, I will."

"Well, I have the vision of a black rider that
continually comes to me in a sort of stupor that
I experience between sleeping and waking. I
cannot describe what I mean nor the feeling of
it. But I know I am not asleep nor yet awake.
The rider is always going along a dark road, and
he comes up and holds out his arms to me. His
face is covered, but I know him. It is the form
of Robert Van Doren. But before I can touch
his hand, he is gone, and when I call out after
him, everything grows utterly black and I am
awake with a terrible misgiving at my heart.

Oh, I am afraid something has happened to him."

The girl seldom let herself out so fully, and Nannie saw that she was terribly wrought up.

"It is nothing, Mary," she said. "You've been brooding too much and it has made you nervous and sleepless. It will all come right if you try not to worry and wonder too much."

"I knew you would say that and I would rather not have told you."

"Don't be offended, dear. What I say is only for the best. It is what Tom would say to you if he were here."

"Yes, that's true, for he would understand no better than you, Nannie. There is with me something more than the dream—a feeling here," she pressed her hand to her breast, " a peculiar ache that isn't so much an ache as a premonition of one. You don't know what I mean, but I do."

"I think I almost understand. It's the same feeling that I have in my feet just before I step on the jack in your father's warehouse."

Mary looked up quickly to see if her friend was joking, but the eyes that met her own were perfectly serious, and though she could not vouch for the correctness of the likeness, she felt that somehow, Nannie understood.

"But," the latter pursued, "I never let the

feeling in my foot get the better of me, and neither must you give way to that in your heart. It may be there, and it may seem something, but just keep on going."

"That's hardly necessary advice," smiled Mary. "It's the one thing that we have to do in life, keep on going. No matter how many presentiments you have, you've got to go on to their fulfillment. That's one thing that gives me the horrors at times until I want to shriek aloud —this unending forward movement. If one could only stop sometimes—but we can't."

"Don't, Mary, don't; there are some things that we must neither think nor talk about, some things that we must leave to a Higher Intelligence than ours."

"But suppose that one does think about them, that one cannot help it—that everything suggests these thoughts?"

"Oh, in that case, one goes out into the open air with me, walks down to the shop, and as she has a quick eye, helps me match some goods," and seeking to divert her mind from the gloomy thoughts that were taking possession of it, Nannie hurried Mary into her hat and out upon the streets.

The day was full of sunshine, but the air was limpid with the suggestion of rain, and a soft breeze blew up from the river. The town was humming and drowsing comfortably, and there was nothing in its appearance to indicate that just a little below the surface there smouldered volcanic fires of discontent and unrest. The whole place was the embodiment of peace. The blinds of the houses were closed to keep out the garish sunlight and the most active sign of life upon the resident streets was the young children playing in the gutters and on the pavements.

Something of the restfulness of the scene possessed Mary and for the time drove the clouds from her mind. The bright day and her forebodings did not set well together. Could it be true that on such a morning as this with such a sky overhead men could be hating each other and seeking each others' lives? Her mind rejected the incongruity. After all, the darkest hour is just before dawn. She had been going through her dark hour and now all the brightness and beauty about her were but the promise of the better time coming. She went into the shop with Nannie stepping lightly and with a smile on her face.

Though poetry has told us that coming events cast their shadows before them, science has not troubled itself to deal largely with this subject of premonition, nor is it believable that those shadows are cast upon all hearts. But there is little doubt that to some there is given the added sorrow of feeling the approach of catastrophe some time before the fact. Call it presentiment or what you will, there are those who are capable of feeling disaster before it comes. Of these, was Mary Waters, and bright as her face had been when she entered the shop with Nannie the clouds had settled upon it again when she emerged.

"Let us walk up Main street," she said, and her companion agreed.

Nannie chatted on cheerfully because she had not noted Mary's return to her former depression. Had she only looked at her companion's gloomy face, her flow of talk would have been checked. Mary's eyes were fastened upon a knot of people surrounding a bulletin board in front of the *Diurnal* office.

"Something is wrong," said Mary suddenly, breaking in on her friend's talk.

"Why do you think so?" asked the surprised girl.

"Look at the crowd up there. Let us go and see."

Reluctantly Nannie complied and they were soon on the outskirts of the growing crowd. They could not get near enough to see the words on the board, but some one read aloud for the benefit of the late comers the words that made Mary pale with terror and turn hastily way.

"John Morgan with his cavalry has crossed the river and is advancing into Ohio."

"John Morgan is in Ohio, and Robert is with him—my vision, the Black Rider." The disjointed words beat time to the throbbing of her heart. "John Morgan is in Ohio and Robert is with him."

The news spread like wildfire and already the town was alive with people hastening to the centre of intelligence. The drowsy summer quiet had gone from the streets as if by magic, and instead there were the shuffling of feet and the babble of many tongues. But Mary did not speak and Nannie gave her the sympathy of silence. Only when they were in the house again did she say, "I shall never question your feelings again. Never." Then with rare good sense, she left Mary to herself.

The shock, coming as it had, as a confirmation of her fears and holding in it unknown possibilities for trouble had a severe effect upon the girl. She was distressed for the safety of her lover, but not only that, for a new element had entered into her feelings. Heretofore, she had had little or no doubt as to the righteousness of her loyalty to Robert. But now it was a very different thing. He was no longer a brave man exiled and driven into the army of the enemy. He was now the invader of his own home and hers.

As long as he fought on the soil of his father's state against invasion, he might still have her love and sympathy; but did he not, by this last act, forfeit both? Reasoning with a woman's narrow vision, she admitted his right to defend himself and those he loved against the government, but questioned his privilege to attack it. It is not to be denied that sentiment had much to do with Mary's point of view. In one rôle, Robert was the prince, in the other, the ogre, and she could not quite reconcile herself to sympathy with the ogre. It was rather a nice question to ask her to decide whether the right of defence did not carry with it the right of attack. There was something of horror in the picture she drew of him, riding a marauder over the fields of the state that had so long sheltered him. In her mind, the whole invasion was narrowed down to one man. It was not Morgan and his men—it was Robert—Robert, for whom she had left home, for whom she had suffered contempt. What did it matter to her that John Morgan was with him? What did it matter to her that he was one of two thousand? Then her trend of thought began to change. Had he not been forced to go where he was? She remembered his words to her father on that memorable night. "The Confederacy may thank you for another recruit!" Must he not do then as his comrades

did? Would it not be cowardice in him to refuse to go where they went? Would he do
wrong consciously? She could not believe it.
After all, she loved him and she would trust him
blindly, whatever happened. The inevitable
thing occurred. Her love triumphed. She need
have asked herself no perplexing questions had
she only begun with, " Is my love for him strong
enough to overlook all shortcomings?" With
Nannie in the same case, it would have been
different. There would have been no questions
at all. She would merely have said, "Well, if
he does it, it must be right," and gone on with
a contented mind. Even Mary was happier for
her decision, though she reached it after much
doubt.

Dorbury heard of the rebel general's daring
dash into Ohio with an astonishment that was
only equalled by its anger and terror. There
had been threats and rumors of some danger
from Kentucky, but the possibility of it had been
beyond belief. Now that the thing had really
come, men stood aghast. Men who had scoffed
before, now became suddenly serious. Men who
had wavered in their allegiance, now spoke out
boldly for the Union when their homes were
menaced. On every side was the cry "The
Home Guards, the Home Guards," and old men,
middle-aged men and beardless youths went

flocking into the armory. "Be sure," said some, "if he dares cross into Ohio, there are more behind him, and it means that they intend to overwhelm the state!" Others said, "They will burn Cincinnati, strike here, unless we can check them, march on and destroy the capital."

On any corner, sane men, fanatics and demagogues could secure audiences to listen to their oratory, in which they adjured their hearers to rise in their might and drive the invader from their sacred soil.

There were some men in the town who smiled and added, "It is a feint, let Morgan come. He will not come far." There were not many of them. There were others who gathered behind the closed blinds of Stephen Van Doren's house to talk of this new development. To them Van Doren spoke confidentially. "I deplore this move," he said. "It will take away sympathy from the cause of the South, although Morgan is only doing what Lincoln has done in the South. It is a sorry matter all through, for we have been plunged into a war that might have been averted by able statesmanship. If worst comes to worst, we have only our government to thank, and yet it is a bad thing, for nothing will do more to cement a feeling of clannishness in the North and give these fanatics something to point to than this same attempt to fight the devil with fire."

Among all the crowding men, the believers in different creeds, walked Bradford Waters like an Elijah among the prophets of Baal. The news was to him as the battle-smoke to the nostrils of the war-horse. He seemed like one inspired, and it was as if the things that he had longed for had been done. There was a look of exaltation on his face, but his was an emotion too deep for words, though none who saw him needed speech of him.

In her bedroom, his daughter sat staring silently out of her window, not thinking—hardly dreaming—and so night fell on Dorbury.

CHAPTER XXI

A VAGUE QUEST

Iᴛ is doubtful how long Mary would have sat staring out into the darkness had not the entrance of Nannie and her preparations for bed disturbed her revery. She also disrobed and was soon lying in bed, her eyes wide open and her thoughts busy with the events of the day. She did not want to talk and so made but brief replies to Nannie's proffers of conversation. Finally, from feigning sleep, she fell into a light doze from which she started crying, "The Black Rider! The Black Rider!"

The experiences of the last few hours had exhausted Nannie, and though it was yet early in the evening, she was sleeping soundly. Mary recovered herself, and finding that she was not observed, crept stealthily from the bed. She paused for awhile beside the window, and then dressed with feverish haste as if spurred by a definite purpose. When she was fully clothed she stepped quietly down the stairway, and past the sitting-room where some of the family were still up, and glided out of the house. Why she was doing so, she herself could not have told, but something was dragging or driving her on, on, towards the station. She had yet no fixed idea where she was going, but she felt in her pocket for money and it never occurred to her until she found the amount of her fare that from the beginning she had intended to go to Cincinnati, though that she did not yet know, the tendency towards a definite act being rather subconscious than apprehended. There was just time to catch the half-past ten train. She reached the station, bought her ticket and sank breathless and dazed into a seat.

There was a moment's delay, and then the train sped away into the darkness. The sum of all her impressions was that the Black Rider whose face was still concealed from her, flitted ever by the side of the coach and just at her window. The lights of the town faded from view and the river lay behind her a line of sinuous silver. The sky overhead was besprent with pale stars, but she saw only the cloaked and muffled man, riding, riding as one rides in a nightmare. The train whistled, wheezed and paused at stations, and then went panting on, and Mary, knowing as little, feeling hardly more than the dumb mechanism that carried her, went on upon a vague, unknown quest, for what, she could not have told.

Prompting her action there was apparently no cause or intelligence. Scarcely was there even volition. Some force, stronger and wiser than she, good or malignant, impelled her forward whether she would or no. She went on not because she would, but because she must.

The night became suddenly overcast, the sky darkened, the stars went out, and as the train flew on its way southward, a peal of thunder broke from the heavens, and sharp rain began pattering against the window. She crouched lower in her seat and stared ever out through the pane where she could see the mantled figure riding, riding. She could hear his horse's hoofbeats above the sound of the storm, and her eyes sought vainly his face, though she knew and could not be deceived in the form.

When the coach drew into Cincinnati, she alighted and still blind, dazed and apparently without direction, hastened out and took a car. The night was one of inky blackness, the rain was coming down in torrents, while intermittent flashes of lightning showed her the wet and shining streets and the roadways through which she was passing. At the call, Avondale, she left the car and went on blindly into the night.

Terror now seized her, terror of the unknown, of the darkness, of the mystery in her own wild act; but she could not stop nor turn back. Was

she fleeing from or to something? Once in a
moment of consciousness, she asked herself the
question, but hurried on without answering or
attempting to answer it. On, through the little
suburban village and out upon a country road, a
mile out; the last house had been passed, the
last light had flickered out of her sight, and then
drenched, exhausted, she paused under a huge oak
and turned her eyes back over the way she had
come. It was not weariness that made her stop,
it was a sense of waiting, waiting for something,
the thing for which she had come. It was perhaps a half hour that she had stood there, and
then the sound of clattering hoofs struck her ear.
She pressed closer to the tree. A company of
cavalrymen were approaching. They came at a
smart canter. Breathlessly, she awaited. They
were near to her. They were passing, first close
together, then with gaps between, then scatter-
ingly. With her physical ear she heard the
sound of their hoof-beats in the soft, slushy mud,
but with her inner sense, she heard the sound of
one horse on dry ground, and her eyes saw but
one rider, still the black mantled figure of her
dreams. She heard him, saw him coming nearer,
nearer, then a flash of lurid lightning lit the
whole scene, and starting forward from the tree,
she cried, "Robert, Robert!"

As if but one man had heard her, as if her

voice had been intended to reach but one, a
figure shrouded in a dark cloak, whirled and rode
from the straggly ranks up to the side of the
road and dismounted. She stretched her arms
out. Another flash of lightning showed the
trooper the white face of the girl beside the tree,
and with a cry he caught her to him as she fell
forward.

"Mary, Mary," he cried, "can it be you? Are
you flesh or spirit? My God, what does it
mean?" But she was lying cold in his arms.
The cavalry passed on, stragglers and all. He
stood there helplessly holding her, one hand
clutching his horse's bridle. The rain from the
leaves dripped in her face, and she revived.

"Robert," she said faintly.

"What are you doing here?" he asked.

"I—I—don't know. I dreamed of you and I
came. Where am I?"

"On the road out of Cincinnati, about two
miles from Avondale. Who came with you?"

"I came alone."

"Where are you going?"

"I don't know. Something sent me to you."

"You are very weak," he said.

"I must go back now," she replied.

"Where will you go?"

"I don't know."

The power that had driven her out, that had

guided her seemed suddenly to have left her helpless and without direction.

The men now were entirely passed, and without a
word, he lifted her to his saddle and springing
up behind her, turned his horse's head back towards the town.

"God knows what brought you here, darling,"
he whispered close to her ear, "but it was something stronger and wiser than us both. It has
been a long, hard ride with me, and I was losing
hold, but you have given me strength again.
People have heard our horses and are aroused, but
I will take you back where you will be safe.
Another day," he bent over and kissed her brow,
"when all of this is over, you shall tell me how
and why you came to me, love of my heart."

She nestled closer to him and did not answer.
There was nothing for her to say, she did not
understand, he did not understand. He rode
straight into the town. Dark forms were gathering upon the corners. Here and there a torch
flared.

"I must leave you now, Mary," he said, "the
power that brought you will care for you. I
must join my company. God be with you."

He set her down and was wheeling away, when
a torch beside him flared. A man cried, "Here's
one of them!"

Van Doren struck spurs to his horse and the

animal dashed away. A hue and cry arose. There was a volley of shots, and the night swallowed the Black Rider. A crowd surrounded Mary and led her speechless and confused to the nearest house. A few of the bolder spirits followed the rider on foot, until the sound of his horse's hoofs had died away into the distance.

The girl could not give any clear account of herself except that she had come from Dorbury and had wandered out of her way. Kind matrons put her to bed where she fell asleep like a child, though she would have rested less easily had she known that Robert was swaying, white-faced in his saddle, his arm shattered by a bullet.

All night long, men full of alarm, patroled the streets of the village fearing and expecting an attack, while women stayed up and brewed tea and talked of their night visitor. When Mary awoke in the morning, the events of the night before were like a dream to her, and though the women questioned her closely and eagerly she was able to give them little or nothing of the satisfaction for which they longed. It was all so strange, so unbelievable, that she did not dare tell them all that had really happened. There were some who said that she must be a spy, and there were threats of detaining her, but she made it clear where she lived, mentioning the names of people whom several of them knew, and so they put her down as some demented or half-witted creature who had lost her way and been rescued by the trooper in grey.

"Well, the hound will have one thing to his credit," said the husband of the woman at whose house she had slept.

Her head clear, the girl was anxious now to return to her home. The busy little matron, still suspecting her sanity, insisted on going with her as far as the train, where with many head-shakes and mysterious comments, she put Mary in charge of the conductor and went away trembling for the safety of her protégée.

The whole Woods household was in an uproar of excitement and Nannie was blaming herself keenly for negligence when Mary walked in.

"Oh, Mary, Mary," cried her friend at sight of her, "where have you been? You've given us such a fright. We've searched everywhere for you."

But Mary only smiled and kept her counsel. "I had to go away," she said.

"What time did you leave?"

Mary smiled again. A little later a message came from Bradford Waters saying, "Have you found Mary yet?"

Nannie blushed. "We thought you had gone home, and so we went there."

"I was not at home," was the only answer.

Whatever it may have meant, the girl herself was never able to explain it, but Mary saw no more visions and she was happier.

The puzzle was deep in Robert's mind as he rode away from the girl, leaving her to the mercies of the gaping townspeople. He had no doubt that they would treat her kindly and send her home in safety. But the thought that held him and made him forget even the pain in his arm that grew and grew was how she had come there. How had she known where to find him, when even the troopers themselves did not know whither they were tending? Who gave the simple, emotional girl the information that the governor of Ohio would have given so much to have? There was nothing in the range of Robert's experience to explain the phenomenon, so although he hugged the memory of her presence to his consciousness, he gave up speculation to wait for that later day when he had said she would tell him. His thoughts now had time to revert to his wound, and he found that his sleeve was soaked with blood that was fast stiffening in spite of the constant downpour. The absorption of his attention no longer kept his misery in subordination. He began to feel fainter and fainter, but clenched his teeth and laid his head upon the neck of his good mare. A mile more, and the sound of moving men came to his ears.

Then he gained upon them faster and knew that they had halted for the night. His head was ringing like a chime of bells. His heart throbbed painfully and his tongue was parched. Heavier and heavier he lay upon the mare's neck, and when finally the animal halted in the hastily improvised camp, it was an inert body that had to be lifted from her back.

Already Mary was quietly sleeping in the friendly house and no dream or vision told her of the lover who was to ride no more with John Morgan, but unknown, was to be nursed back to life by a good-hearted farmer and his wife.

CHAPTER XXII

THE HOMECOMING OF THE CAPTAIN

THROUGH the newspapers, and an occasional letter from the field, Bradford Waters was kept advised of the movements of his son. With his regiment, he had taken part in the engagements at Pittsburg Landing, and in all the active operations of the Army of Ohio, or, as it was finally rechristened, the Army of the Cumberland. He had distinguished himself in the terrible fight of the 19th of July, and it was as a captain that he lay with his company at Chattanooga Creek, encouraging his men by example not to flinch under the awful fire which the Confederate batteries poured upon them.

Dorbury knew the privations through which her boys were going, the long marches when both rest and refreshment were denied, the hardships of camp and field and the heroism of patient endurance. Then began that gradual turn of sentiment and feeling for which the battle of Pittsburg Landing and Morgan's raid had proved the cue. Another wave of enthusiasm for her patriotic sons swept over the town, and this time, had permanent effect. Even Davies scoffed no longer and spoke of "our boys" in a tone that led Waters to forgive all his past transgressions.

Tom had always been a favorite at home, but men spoke his name now with a new affection. After each new engagement in which his regiment was known to have taken a part, there were numerous inquiries at the Waters house as to how "the captain" had fared. He was no longer a family idol. He had become a public hero.

This pride in a young man's success, is, after all, of the vanity which is human. Something of credit seems to accrue to the man himself when he can say, " What! Captain ———, why I knew him when he was a boy! "

Behind closed doors, Stephen Van Doren sat and read the papers. He had the largeness of heart that made him respect a brave man wherever placed, and now he felt a real pride in the son of his enemy. To be sure, in his heart, he had misgivings and wished time and again that he might read something of his own son of whose whereabouts he knew nothing. There had come one brief letter some time before the raid, and since that, nothing. Why couldn't his Bob be a captain, too? His anxiety was shared in some degree by Mary, but the pride which she took in her brother and which Nannie constantly nourished, left her little time for brooding.

The summer wore away amid rumors of battles, reconnoissances, and skirmishes. The golden autumn came, and although so many of the husbandmen were away reaping strange harvests in a strange land, the land smiled with the fullness of things, and the ring of scythes could be heard afield. Over the little town, over the fair meadows that surrounded it, the sun of plenty hung and drove away the darkness that the preceding summer had known. Morgan had come and gone and they felt no fear of another such invasion. Terror was dead and the people bent themselves joyously to the task of supplying whatever wants those at the front expressed. They rested in a content and security that even the imminence of a battle at Mission Ridge in which their "Own" might be engaged failed wholly to destroy. Orchard Knob had dealt kindly with them, and they began to think of their soldiers as each an Achilles with the vulnerable heel secure. Then like a tempest from a cloudless sky came the news of the battle of November 25th, and Dorbury was silent from sheer amazement. Could this thing really have happened to them and theirs? They looked down the list of the dead and wounded again. So many of the names were familiar. So many were those whom they thought to see again. Tom Waters, Captain Tom, could it be? Their young hero? They began to awake, and with the awakening the place became as a house of mourning. The bulletin boards were surrounded by hushed, awe-stricken men, while women with white faces, hastened up to hear the latest from the field.

It was Davies, who having heard the news, went over to break it to Bradford Waters. He had not left his office at the warehouse, and only knew from vague rumors that a battle had taken place. He was hastening through to get out and hear the particulars, when Davies entered, his white face speaking for him before his lips could utter a sound. Waters sprang to his feet, and then sank back into a chair.

"There has been a battle, they tell me," he said.

"Yes," said Davies, with dry lips.

"Was—was—Tom's name mentioned?" He asked the question mechanically as if he already knew the answer that was coming.

Davies was trembling, the tears filled his eyes as he went over and laid his hand on the other's shoulder.

"Yes," he answered. "Tom—the captain's name, Waters, is among the killed."

An ashen pallor spread over Waters' seamed

face and his hard hands gripped the desk in front of him fiercely. He breathed heavily but did not speak.

"Come, Bradford, come out in the air with me."

Waters rose, but there was a knock at the door, and opening it a messenger confronted him. It was a telegram from Tom's colonel. The old man could hardly read the words, his hand trembled so. But he made out that they were sending him home. Then Davies saw the man's form straighten up and his eye flash as with a clear voice he read, "Killed, while leading a gallant charge." "Thank God, Davies, he died like a soldier."

There was not a tear in Waters' eye, though pride and grief struggled for mastery in his voice. Davies, who under all his cynical indifference was as soft-hearted as a woman, was weeping like a child.

"I gave him unreservedly," the bereaved father went on, "and he has given me nothing to regret. Come on, I must go home, I must set my house in order to receive my son, the captain."

They went out of the house together, Bradford Waters' face set and firm. Men looked at him shyly upon the street and greeted him briefly. They knew how deeply he had loved his son, and feared a break down of his self-control. Men are always cowards in the face of grief. But their caution was unnecessary. Waters returned their civility with a poise of manner almost stern. What had he to weep for? He had laid his son upon the altar, and he had proven an acceptable sacrifice. Other men might weep for craven sons who had left the fighting to others or who had trembled under fire. As for him, he must be strong. He must walk among men with a high head and a step that showed him worthy to be the father of such a son.

Davies left him at the door of his house. He heard him say as he entered, "You must look sharp, Martha, and have everything in good order. The captain is coming home."

The light was fast fading from the room where Waters sat down, but a ray of gold came in through the window and touched the pictured face of the dead soldier in its place on the mantel. The father rose and taking it down held it close to his breast. "I gave you to them, boy," he murmured, "and they took you, but they cannot, they can never take the memory of you from me."

Some one knocked, and a moment later Martha came in, saying, "A gentleman to see you, Mr. Waters."

With perfect self-possession he passed into the

next room, where in the dimness a man stood awaiting him.

"I have dared to come, Bradford," said Stephen Van Doren's voice, "because I knew, and we both loved the boy. I thought maybe we could shake hands over the memory of a brave soldier."

Waters' form trembled like an aspen. He paused in silence, and the moment was full of import. It was to say what the course of his whole future life would be. Whether the iron of his nature would be melted or annealed by the fire through which he was passing. He took a step forward and grasped Van Doren's outstretched hand.

"I am glad you came, Stephen," he said; "he was a brave boy, and you loved him, too."

"No one could help loving him. He was one man among a thousand who was fine enough for the sacrifice. Whether my son be alive or dead, may I always have as little right to sorrow for him as you have for yours to-night."

Stephen Van Doren's voice was low, earnest and impressive, and it broke down something that had stood up very hard and stern in Bradford Waters' spirit. The tears welled up into his eyes and fell unheeded down his cheeks. He wrung Van Doren's hand.

"You must stay and talk to me of him, of both

of them. Our boys fought on different sides, Stephen, but they were both ours."

"In a time like this, before an example of bravery, we forget sides and differences and only remember our boys and our love for them."

For awhile they sat and talked of the dead, and of him of whose whereabouts they as yet knew nothing, and Waters' heart was lightened and softened.

"You must go away," he said at last to his visitor, "I have another thing that I must do. Maybe, after all, Stephen, there is a deeper meaning in this sacrifice than either of us yet sees."

"May God grant it," was the fervent response.

"When you hear from Bob, let me know at once. You know he was Tom's friend," he added, almost joyously.

As soon as Van Doren was gone, he gave the servant some directions, and then set out for Nathan Woods' house, which was no less than his own a place of bereavement. The entire household was grief-stricken. The two girls had mingled their tears and sought vainly to comfort each other in their sorrow. Mary was fairly exhausted from her grief, and Nannie, seeing that, recovered herself sufficiently to minister to the weaker girl.

When Mary found out that her father was below and asking for her, she sprang up with wild eyes and fluttering heart.

"Oh, he has come to reproach me," she said. "He will never forgive me."

"There is no reproach in his face, Mary. I think he wants you to be with him when Tom comes home."

Nannie's voice reassured her, and together they went down hand in hand. When his daughter came into the room, Bradford Waters held forth his arms, and with a cry that was half grief, half joy, she flung herself into them.

"Father, father," she sobbed, "what shall we do without him?"

"What would his country have done without him, my dear? It has taken him, and we must give him ungrudgingly."

Nannie was leaving the room, but with a new softness, a quality his voice had never known, he put out his hand to her.

"Come, my other daughter," he said, "you loved him too."

For the three, then, there was no past, no difference, no wrong. They were all members of one family bound more strongly by a great love and a great grief. There was a strange similarity apparent in the attitude of Nannie and Bradford Waters towards Tom's death. While Mary thought almost solely of the brother she had lost, they both seemed to say, "We are glad to give him, since we may give him thus."

"Come, let us go home," said Waters, "there is much to do. Mary, come. Nannie, you must go with us. We must go and make ready to receive the captain."

And together they went with him to receive the captain.

The strange idea took Bradford Waters to prepare for his son's homecoming as if the dead could know. Perhaps there did remain to him some of the mysticism to which his New England birth and ancestry gave him right. It would not have assorted illy with his bleak nature. Perhaps he believed that Tom would know. However it was, he had determined that all should be quite as the young man would have liked it had he come home with conscious eyes to see and light with pleasure at what he saw.

To Mary the house was very desolate, and a rush of sad emotions swept over her as she looked at the familiar things arranged by an alien hand.

"Tom would hardly know the place now, if he could see it," she told her father.

But he replied, "Never mind, never mind, it shall all be set right before he comes. He shall find nothing to his distaste."

The saddest duty they had was the arrangement of his room. The old man still followed his strange whim, and had the chamber arranged as if a living guest were to occupy it. The bed was laid as Tom would have had it laid, and the fresh sheets turned back as if to receive his tired form. In the vases was the late golden-rod, always a great favorite with him. But on his pillows were the marks of tears which Nannie had shed as she smoothed their soft whiteness, and knew that his brown head would never press them again.

To her a great change had come. In spite of the pride and fortitude which bore her up, the light and spontaneity had gone out of her life. She might laugh again, but it would never be with the old free ring. In spirit, she was already Tom's wife, and she was now as much widowed as any woman who had followed her husband to the grave. That she bore her burden better than Mary, was largely due to the practical strength of her love for Tom. Had he lived, she would have been glad to welcome and help him. As he was dead, she was no less his and waited the time when she might join him. Mary might weep for him, but she would wait for him, believing that no such love as hers was given to mortals to wither and die without fruition. This love held her so utterly above ordinary opinions and conventions that she did not think to ask what would be said of her entering her lover's house as one of the family. It was nothing to her. It was a matter of course. There was a certain joy in feeling that she had the right to help and in seeing hour after hour that Tom's father and sister leaned more and more upon her strength.

It was on the third day after the news of the battle that Tom's body was brought home, one mute mourner accompanying it—Nigger Ed. Those were strenuous times and there was no opportunity for fine courtesies, for escorts and officer pall-bearers, even for that brave one, but the flag was wrapped around him, the flag he had fought and died for.

His father was very calm as he looked at the boyish face so cold and still before him. Death had been kind to the soldier and had come quickly, leaving him almost unaltered. He lay as if he had fallen asleep with bright dreams of a purposeful to-morrow. There was none of the horror or dread of battle impressed upon his marble countenance, nothing that could cause the woman who loved him best of all to shrink from him.

Bradford Waters stooped and kissed his son's brow. There was a smile on his own lips. Even Mary forgot to weep. This was the majesty, the beauty of death. Nannie hovered over him as she would over a flower. They were alone together—these three, when a knock, soft and hesitating, fell upon the door. Bradford opened it to find without the negro Ed. He silently motioned him to enter.

"Dey tol' me to gin you dis when you was settled," he said. He handed Waters a letter. It was from Colonel Bassett, Tom's commanding officer, and ran,

"Dear Sir, I wish I knew how to pay tribute to the finest man and most gallant gentleman I ever knew—your son. I wish I might have shown him the respect that I feel and come with his body to see it laid in its last resting-place, but this is war. I would condone with you, sir, but that I know the father of such a son must be proud to have had him die where and as he did."

It was a soldier's letter and though Waters read it with trembling voice, his eyes glowed and he looked at the still form as if to say, " I would not have had it otherwise."

Ed was still standing, waiting for the father to speak. But Waters said nothing. The negro shifted uneasily, then he said anxiously, " Is you mad at me, Mistah Watahs ? Has de cunnel said anythin' ? Dey wouldn't have sont me home wid him, but I baiged, 'cause I kinder thought you'd ravah have somebody—dat knowed him— bring him back."

Waters reached out and grasped the black

man's hand. "Why, God bless you forever and ever," he said.

The privacy of the family even with its dead could not long be maintained. Dorbury had suspended business. This hero was theirs as well as his family's. They filled the sidewalks, they surged at the doors. They would see him. They would bring their flowers to lay beside his bier. He belonged to them, to them, who had helped to send him forth and had cheered his departure. Bradford Waters should not be selfish in his grief. The boys from the factories and warehouses came, and also from the shops, those who had known him and those who had not. All men know a hero. And the father said, "Let them come in, he will be glad to see them."

And so "the captain" came home.

CHAPTER XXIII

A TROUBLESOME SECRET

FOR a long time curiosity was rampant in a little country district not very far from Cincinnati. It was the proverbial rural locality where every one knows or wishes to know the business of every one else, and is offended if he doesn't. In this particular place, the object of interest was a white farmhouse set forward on the road, and fronting ample grounds both of field and garden. It was the home of John Metzinger, a prosperous German husbandman and his good wife, Gretchen. They were pleasant, easy-going people, warm-hearted and generous. Their neighbors had always looked upon them with favor, until one day—it was early in August, the eye of suspicion fell upon the house. Those who had lived near the Metzingers, and those who merely passed upon the road to and from town began to point questioning fingers at the place and to look askance at it. The gossips shook their heads and whispered together.

It all began with one woman who had unceremoniously "dropped in" on the couple; "dropping in" consisting of pushing open the door and entering unannounced by the formality of a knock. The easy-going neighbor had pursued this course only to find the door of an inner room hastily closed and the good wife profuse in embarrassed expostulations. Mrs. Metzinger was not good at dissimulation, and her explanation that the room was all torn up for she was house-cleaning served but to arouse her visitor's suspicion. In her own words as she told it many times later, she said with fine indignation, "Think o' her sayin' to me that she was cleanin' house, an' she with as spick an' span a white apern on as ever you see. Says I to her, 'Ain't you pickin' out a funny time to clean, Mrs. Metzinger?' and she says with that Dutch brogue o' hers, 'Oh, I cleans anydimes de place gets dirty.' Then I says ca'm like, because I've allus liked that woman, 'I should think you'd get yer apern dirty,' an' all of a sudden she jerked it off an' stood there grinnin' at me; but that was what give her away, for lo, an' behold, her dress was as clean as my bran' new calico. Then I says, 'Well, never min', I'll just come in an' help you,' an' would you believe it, that woman got right in my way an' wouldn't let me go in that room, all the time jabbering something about 'Nod troublin' me.' Right then an' there, thinks I, there's something wrong in that room."

She closed her remarks as one who says, "There's murder behind that door."

Her hearers were struck by her tragic presentation of the case, and they too, began to watch for signs of guilt in the Germans. These were soon plentiful. None was more convincing than that a room that had always been open to the light had now its blinds closed. Some one had said too, that they had seen the doctor's gig at the door one night, and had waited for him to come out. But on questioning him, as any man has a right to do, "Who's sick, doctor?" he had sprung into his vehicle, put whip to his horse and dashed away without answering. This in itself, looked dark. For why should a doctor of all men, refuse to be questioned about his patients? The little scattered community for three or four miles and even further up and down the road was awe-struck and properly indignant. Such communities have no respect for reticence.

Meanwhile the trouble went on, and the Metzingers grew in disfavor. What had been friendly greetings degenerated into stiff nods or grew into clumsily veiled inquiries. While their neighbors lost sleep asking each other what horror was going on behind those closed doors, the simple couple went on about their duty and kept their counsel. It was really not so much the horror that the community resented but that the particulars of it were being kept from them.

If the Metzingers could have told their story, it would have proved, after all, a very short and simple one. It would have been to the effect that late one night towards the end of July, they had been awakened by the tramping of feet and a knocking upon their door. Going thither, they had found four men unkempt and mud-stained, who bore between them another, evidently wounded. They had brought him and laid him upon the sofa, and then with promises, that were half threats, had left him in their care. They came then to know who their visitors were; some of "Morgan's terrible men." Their promises to respect the farmer's stock had not been needed to secure attention for their wounded comrade, for the good wife's heart had gone out already to the young fellow who lay there so white and drabbled with blood.

John Metzinger would have told, though his good wife would never have mentioned it, how all that night and the next day, Gretchen had hovered over the wounded man, bandaging his arm, bathing it, and doing what she could to ease the pain, while the sufferer muttered strange things in his sleep and tossed like a restless child.

They could not get a doctor until the next night, for they knew that all must proceed with secrecy, and when the physician came, the fever had already set in and the chances for the man's recovery seemed very slight.

They could have told too, of the doctor's long fight with the fever, and what the gossips did not know, how one night two physicians came and amputated the wounded arm at the elbow. Then of the long fight for life through the hot August days, of the terrible nights when Death seemed crowding into the close room and the sufferer lay gasping for breath. But they told nothing. Silently they went their way, grieved by the distrust of those about them, but unfaltering in their course. And when Van Doren first looked up weakly enough into the German woman's face, his eyes full of the gratitude he could not speak, both she and her John were repaid for all that they had suffered.

The woman fell upon her knees by the bedside saying, "Dank Got, dank Got, he vill gid vell now, Shon," and "Shon" who was very big and very much a man, pressed his wife's hand and went behind the door to look for something that was not there.

With the cooler weather of autumn came more decided convalescence to the young trooper, but the earliest snows had fallen before he was able to creep to the door that looked out upon the road. He was only the shadow of his former self. Mrs. Metzinger looked at him, full of pity.

"I guess you petter led de toctor wride by your home now. Dey vill vant to hear from you."

"Not yet, not yet," he protested. "It would cause my father too much anxiety, and some others perhaps, too much joy to know how I am faring."

"Your poor fader, dough, he vill be vorried aboud you."

"Father knows the chances of war and he will not begin to worry yet. It would grieve him so much more to know that I am out of it all so soon."

"Mister Robert," said the woman impressively, "you don't know faders. Dey vas yoost like modders, pretty near, und modders, alvays vants to know; if he is vell, she is glad und she dank Got for dat. If he is det, she vants to gry und gry ofer dose leedle shoes dot he used to vear."

"He shall know, he shall know, Mrs. Metzinger, and very soon, for I am going home to him and his joy will make him forget how long he has waited."

"Yes, I guess maype dot is so."

Robert had divined more by instinct than by

any outward demonstration of his hosts that his secret stay in the house had aroused in their neighbors some sort of feeling against these people. He was perfectly sure that should he write to his father, he would come to him in spite of everything, and at any stir or unusual commotion about the house, what was only smouldering now might burst into flame. So, although it wrung his heart to do so, living within sixty miles of his father, he kept his lips closed and gave no sign. His heart had gone out to these people who had sacrificed so much for him, and he wanted to do something in return for them. At first, because of his very weakness, they had forborne to question him about his home and people, and when he was strong enough to act, he had unconsciously accepted this silence as his sacrifice, without divining that he was not the real sufferer, not the real bearer of the burden.

He had promised that he would go home soon, but the case had been a severe one, and it was December before he dared to venture out beyond the gate. Sometimes, when the days were warm and bright, he would sit wrapped up on the porch at the side, for the need of secrecy gone, the Metzingers were openly and humanly unhumble. They bowed proudly, even jauntily to their detractors, while the priest and the Levites passed by on the other side. There were no good Samaritans about save the Metzingers themselves, and their little devices might have gone unobserved, but that the priest and the Levites were curious people, and at last, came over to question.

"Who is the sick young man?" they questioned.

"He iss a friend of ours from de var," Mrs. Metzinger answered them.

"We'd like to talk to him," they volunteered.

"No, he must not talk to beoples, not yet," was the answer.

"Why don't he wear his uniform?" Robert wore a suit of "Shon's" jeans.

"It was yoost ruint and all spoilt mit blood."

But they looked at Robert askance, and the gossip which for awhile from inaction had faltered, sprang up anew. Who was he? Why so little about him? Why had they kept the secret so long?

The good people saw with dismay what they had done. They had only aroused the trouble which they had hoped to allay. Van Doren saw their trouble and determined immediately to relieve them.

"I am going home now," he told them one day.

"You are not yet so strong."

"Oh, yes I am. I'm quite a giant now."

"Vat you dinks Shon? Iss he strong enough?"

"I dinks he gan stay here so long as he vants."

"But I am going, my good friends, it's best for us all."

"Vy?"

"I have seen how the neighbors look at me and I have seen how they look at you. You shan't hurt yourselves any longer."

"Dat iss not right. We care nodings for de neighbors. Ve minds our own business."

Mrs. Metzinger's husband said something under his breath, only a word it was, but it made his wife gasp and cry, "Shon, for shame on you!"

"I'm going," Robert went on, "either with your consent or without. I don't know how I'm ever going to thank you. You've both been so good. It's nasty in a case like this to think of pay. I can't do it decently, but I'm going to do it. It's the nearest way a brute of a man can come to showing his appreciation."

"No pay," said John.

"Not vun cent," said his wife.

"Ve had some gompany," Gretchen put in.

Robert smiled on; they were so like big children.

"I am not going to let you two cheat me out of showing my gratitude by any such excuse."

Gretchen wept and John caused his wife to exclaim again, but it was of no use, and just at dusk, the old carryall took him away to the station, still in his host's suit, the empty sleeve turned up, and the stump of arm flapping at his side.

It was about an hour after John had gone with Robert to the station, that Mrs. Metzinger heard footsteps, and going to the door saw several men without.

"We want that man that's stayin' here," said the leader.

"He's yoost gone to his home in Dorbury."

"In Dorbury—why we thought—what side was he on?"

Mrs. Metzinger drew herself up in dignified anger and said, "I don'd dink Got has any sides, Deacon Callvell," then she slammed the door, and the deacon and his "Committee" went away feeling small, and glad that it was dark, while Mrs. Metzinger rocked out her pious anger until the floor cried again.

CHAPTER XXIV

ROBERT VAN DOREN GOES HOME

THERE was no blare of trumpets, no popular acclaim to greet Robert Van Doren's homecoming. He entered Dorbury alone and unwelcomed, weary and sick at heart. It was half-past eight o'clock when his train drew into the familiar station, and the winter night had settled heavy and black. A familiar form came towards him as he walked down the platform, and sadly changed as he was, he saw the light of recognition in the man's eyes. The next instant, he was looking at the stern lines of an averted face. He shuddered and hurried on as rapidly as his weakness would allow. Although he had often in his moments of convalescence pictured dimly how he would be received at home, yet the actuality was so much stronger and harsher than any anticipation of it could be that he was quite unmanned. For the first time it came to him that he was an alien in the land of his adoption, and even upon the dark streets, he shrank from the people he met because he knew his face would be to them as a leper's, and even the empty sleeve, the badge of honor to so many of them, would read only to these people, " Unclean, unclean."

He was bending his steps towards his father's house, absorbed in bitter thoughts, when a sort of divination, rather than the appearance of things roused him from his revery. He looked around upon the place, the houses, the lawns, and then a lighted window caught his eye and he realized that he was passing Bradford Waters' house.

" I wonder if she is back at home?" he said. " I caused her so much grief." He passed through the gate, and crept up to the window. The light shone through a thin shade, but he could see nothing within the house. After a short while, however, he heard the sound of women's voices, and one was hers. Without warning, all the pent-up feeling of the past three years burst forth in the cry, " Mary ! "

" What's that ? " cried some one within, but there was no answer save the hurried tread of feet across the floor. Aware of what he had done, he was hurrying away, when the front door was thrown open, and he saw her before him standing in a flood of light. Then he could not go. He stood transfixed until she walked down the steps to him crying, " Robert, Robert, I was sure you would come ! " And all he could do was to bow his head and murmur, " Thank God."

She took him by the hand and led him into the house, he unresisting.

" Here is Robert," she said to Nannie. " Did I not tell you he would come ? "

" Yes, and I am glad with you." Her greeting of Robert was tender, almost sisterly. As soon as she could do so tactfully, she left the room, and Van Doren's glance followed her questioningly. He could not understand her subdued manner, her sad face. Mary saw the look in his eyes and asked,

" Do you not know, then ? "

" No," he answered, " what is it ? "

" Tom."

" Tom—not—dead ? "

" Dead, yes."

" Killed ? "

" Yes, at Mission Ridge, nearly a month ago," and she told of all that had happened, while he sat like one dazed.

Finally he broke in, " Tom dead, I living, why is this ? Why this choice of the brave instead of the lukewarm, the soldier instead of the raider ? "

" Robert, Robert, you are not yourself. I weep for my brother, but you, I have you still."

For answer he raised his empty sleeve.

"Ah, Robert, you don't know. I love you. Here are two arms—yours."

He kissed her cheek silently, and then a sound made them start apart and stare into each other's faces with parted lips. Some one was on the step. There was but one person whom it could be.

"Quick, quick," said Mary, opening a door into the next room. "In here." And Robert hurried in just as Bradford Waters entered, finding Mary troubled and embarrassed. He stood looking at her with a sad face, and then he said,

"Mary, you grieve me very much. Has all the past been so hard that you cannot forget it? Has not the past month proven that I am a changed man and that you need hide nothing from me?"

"Yes, father, forgive me." And going to the door she called, "Robert!"

Van Doren came in with a defiant look on his face which vanished at sight of Waters' outstretched hand.

"Why—why—Mr. Waters," he stammered confusedly.

"Yes, yes, I know, my boy, but I'm glad to see you back, Robert."

Robert grasped the old man's hand and wrung it warmly. "I'm so glad you're reconciled to me, you didn't like me before."

"No more of that, no more of that. I always liked you, but I didn't like your principles. I've seen sorrow though, and I look at things differently."

"Mary has told me and it grieved me much."

"You know then, that the captain has come home?"

"Yes, would to God that I might have come like that."

"Tut, tut, have you been home?"

"No, I was on my way there, when I heard Mary's voice and stopped."

"You must go to him at once now, he will be overjoyed."

"Do you think I dare go to him myself? I'm afraid he thinks me dead."

"I have no doubt. Let Mary go with you and break the news to him. Go on."

Mary hastened to put on her hat and cloak, and together the two went out, leaving the old man standing by the mantel looking at them with strange tenderness. Robert turned at the door and looked back. "You will never know what you have done, Mr. Waters, to make my homecoming less than a tragedy to me," he said huskily.

"It was Tom, not I," said Waters gently.

The house looked very dismal as Mary and

Robert approached it, and the latter's heart failed him.

"Has my father seemed to grieve much?" he asked.

"He has been absorbed and preoccupied, but his faith was like mine. We knew you would come back."

"I have heard of the faith that is stronger than death, but I always thought it a meaningless phrase until now. Bless you both."

Stephen Van Doren was drowsing by his library fire when Mary was admitted, but with the courtesy of his kind, he rose and went nimbly to meet her, apologizing meanwhile for his dressing-gown and slippers.

"But, my dear child," he exclaimed, "what brings you here at this hour?"

"Mr. Van Doren," Mary faltered, her face all aglow.

"Stop," he exclaimed, "whether the dead can come to life or not, no girl can show a face like that, unless she has seen her lover. What is it?"

"I have seen him, he is here in the hall."

Van Doren took a step forward, and then stood trembling, but Robert had thrown the door open and rushed to his father.

"Father!"

"My boy!"

This was in the days before men grew too old

to embrace their fathers, and bearded cheeks and lips met. The father's arms were about his son and the empty sleeve fell under his hand. He held it up and then pushed his son from him. His head drooped sadly for a moment, but there was a look of exaltation on his face.

"Father—father, don't let that grieve you. I—I—lost it honorably."

Stephen Van Doren's head went up like a bull's when he scents resistance. "Grieve me," he cried, and then turning to Mary, he said, "Now, my dear, I can show your father that and talk to him upon more nearly equal terms. Why, boy, you've won your spurs, if you haven't got them. To us of the newer land, an empty sleeve, when gallantly won is what the Victoria Cross is to an Englishman."

Robert flushed and moved away a pace further from his father. "But you do not know all."

"All? You said it was won honestly—that is enough."

The young soldier looked appealingly at Mary. "I shall have to tell you all," he said.

"I will go, Robert," she said; "it was wrong for me to stay so long, but this meeting has given me such joy as I have never known before." She turned towards the door.

"You must not go," he cried, detaining her, "it is for you also to know. It belongs to you."

"To me?"

"To you—yes."

"How?"

"You remember that night of nights," he asked her softly. "Do they know of it?"

"No, I have never dared to tell them so wild a story."

"I will tell it now, then."

"You may, Robert, they will believe you, every one will."

Then briefly Robert told his father of the strange meeting with Mary that had resulted in his wound. "I don't know what you will say," he ended, "and I don't know what it means."

"It means God," said his father solemnly. "He sent her. Think of it as an old man's fancy if you will, but he lighted one of his own torches at the moment that you might see each other's faces."

"Oh, Robert," cried Mary. "Then it was for me?"

"Yes, darling. Father forgive us, but Mary is glad."

"Why, Mary, child, you show more sense than that great hulking, one-armed hero."

"Hero—father!"

"The man who is old enough to have done a noble deed and is not old enough to know it, should be sent into a closet like a child."

"He does know it—he must know it. Robert, you must see it."

"Hero" was the word running through young Van Doren's brain and he did not understand. He felt Mary's arms about him, he felt his father's hand pressing his own and his thoughts grew hazy. "Hero," how could he be a hero when he was lying helpless when the best fighting was going on, when—though he dared not say it—he did not even know if his heart were wholly with the cause.

His father's voice broke in upon his revery. "Bob, you are the—well, look here, don't you see what kind of a man he must be who dares to ride away from his comrades and into the face of the enemy, and alone, to save a woman?"

"Yes, don't you see, Rob?" said Mary eagerly.

"Why, I loved her," said Robert. "I loved her, and forgive me, father, more than my cause."

"Unless you had had that in you that made your cause strong and noble, you could not have done it even for love."

"Have I pleased you?"

"I am proud to be your father."

"And Mary, I didn't want to tell you—are you hurt?"

"Hurt with the sort of a hurt that a woman —" she started impulsively towards her lover and then paused abashed.

"Never check a good impulse," said old Van Doren. "I am now looking at the portrait of my grandfather."

The two young people improved the opportunity. The old man showed consideration in the length of time he spent admiring the portrait. But a hurried knock on the door recalled their attention.

A servant with a frightened face entered. "There's a lot of men at the door," he said.

"What do they want?" asked Van Doren sternly.

"They—they say that there is a rebel in here, and they want him."

"Go back to them and say," said the old man, his voice ringing like a trumpet, "that there is no rebel here, but a soldier and the son of a soldier, and if they want to see him, he is at their service when he knows their business with him." The servant retired.

"The hounds have begun to bay already," said Robert, his face set and dogged, though he patted Mary's hair as she clung fearfully to him.

"The hounds!" said his father, bringing from his desk a brace of pistols that had seen service, "you mean the curs. The hounds know their true game. Can you use your left hand?"

"As well as my right."

The father tried vainly to hide his satisfaction

as he handed his son a weapon. Outside a clamor arose, which grew louder and louder, and the servant came flying back. "They say you must come out."

"So they are afraid to chance it where there's a man's chance," said Robert. "Come, father, let us go to them. You are right, they are curs, not hounds, after all."

Mary moved forward with them.

"No, dear, stay here."

"I will not, Robert, I have no fear for myself. I am going with you. If you die, I do not want to live. I am going."

"Think of your father."

"Do you think of my brother? Would he have me do less?"

The cries were growing fiercer every moment, and the father at the door cried, "Come on," and stepped out as if eager to meet a crowd of enthusiastic admirers. They passed along the hall, threw open the front door and stepped out into the blaze of light which fell from the chandelier within. At their appearance a hoarse cry rose from the lips of the mob, for mob it was, low, ignorant, infuriated.

"There he is—the rebel!"

"Rebel's too good for him—copperhead's the name!"

"Traitor!"

"Coward!"

They stood calmly upon the steps, the three. Robert, pale but dauntless; his father as fixed as a statue, and Mary just behind them, like a spirit of Justice, with eyes unbound.

When their attitude had somewhat quieted the tumult, Stephen Van Doren spoke, and his voice was calm and hard. "Well, gentlemen," he said, "what is it that you want of us?"

"We want your son. We want that damned copperhead that's joined the rebels and been killing our boys. That's what we want," came the reply in fifty voices.

"There is no traitor and no copperhead here," Van Doren went on. "My son, it is true, is here," and he bowed to Robert as if he were delivering a complimentary address, "but he is none of the things which you name. He is a man who has fought for his convictions, and has returned here where he has as good a right as any of you. He is here, I say, and if any or all of you want him, damn you, come and take him!"

The old man's voice had risen, and at the moment both he and Robert, as if by a preconcerted signal, raised their pistols and levelled them at the foremost ranks of the mob. Intimidated at this defiance, the crowd fell back. Just then a rock hurtled past Van Doren's head, and crashed through a window. The noise was like an electric shock to the rabble's failing energies, and with the cry, "Come on, rock them!" they started forward again, those behind forcing the front ranks.

"Try not to kill any of the fools," the father whispered briefly to his son.

They were both pressing their triggers and the forward men were on the first step, when a new cry, "Waters, Waters!" checked their advance, and a man with flowing white hair who had been thrusting his way through the crowd, also mounted the step. The mob thought it had found a new champion, and again yelling, "Waters, Waters!" rushed forward, but Waters turned and faced them, waving his arms.

"Back, back, you cowards!" he cried. They paused in amazement, as he backed slowly up the steps. When they took in his meaning, they attempted another rush, but he stood above them, and suddenly from beneath his coat he tore a long whip with leaden tipped thongs.

"Back," he cried, wielding it with terrific force into the faces and over the heads of the leaders. "Take this, this is for dogs. Back to your kennels, I say!"

His face was terrible, and the men in front quickly turned and began fighting their way to the rear. Others followed, and a panic seized upon them. When Waters stood alone, and the mob at a safe distance began sullenly to gather, some one shouted, "If it wasn't for your son's sake, Waters, we'd kill you."

Waters indicated that he wished to speak, and they became silent with the silence of watchful beasts.

"If it were not for my son's sake!" he said. "I gave him for the cause of right and decency, and I am willing to give myself. What right has any of you who joins so cowardly an attack as this to take upon his lips the name of a brave man? Let never a man who was in .this mob to-night utter my son's name again, or by the God who rules over us, I will kill him!" A breath like a shudder passed over the rabble, and Waters went on, "I have lost and I have the right to demand the full worth of my sacrifice, and you who know my loss, have no right to deny me this." He moved up beside Robert, and putting his hand on his shoulder, said, "This man shall stand to me in lieu of the son I have lost, and his empty sleeve shall be the sign of an eternal compact between us, the badge of honor which it is. He is mine, not yours. Mine, by the blood of my son, mine by the void in my heart. Touch him, if you dare! Go home," and he began moving down the steps, his whip grasped tightly in his hand. "Go home, I say, or I'll whip you there."

The mob fell back, and just then the orderly tramping of feet was heard and a rush was made in an opposite direction as the police arrived on the scene, late and reluctant.

The four turned and went silently into the house. They sat silent, too, in the library, all too tense for speech, until Waters said, " Come, Mary, let us go. You need have no fear of further trouble, Bob, the captain will be about. Steve, I disagree with you very much in your last article in the *Diurnal*. You are all wrong, but I'll talk to you about that to-morrow. Good-night. Come, Mary. It is strange how fanatical some men will be on a subject."

CHAPTER XXV

CONCLUSION

In the after days, it was as Bradford Waters had said, and Robert Van Doren experienced no further trouble at the hands of the mob. Indeed, no man was willing to be known as having been a member of the party. When it was talked about in public, men turned their faces away and did not meet each others' eyes. In so small a town, it was inevitable that many of the participants in such an affair should be known, but no name was ever mentioned, and the matter was not pressed. However, there was something suspicious about the manner in which some men avoided Bradford Waters, and kept silent when others spoke his son's name.

In the close counsels which took place between the two families, formerly so far apart, Robert had suggested that perhaps it would be better for him to go away from Dorbury to some place where he was not known; but both Waters and his father strenuously objected to that.

"No," said the latter, "there are times when

concessions must be made to the prejudices of people. There are other times when it is no less than righteous to ride them down."

"Your father is right. Had I lived in the South with my early training and bent of thought, I should have had no better sense than to stand up for my principles just as he did. I should have resented any Southerner's question of my right to do so. The trouble with us all is that we will not allow others the right which we demand for ourselves."

"I think the trouble with us all is that we talk a great deal about free thought and free speech, meaning that others shall have both as long as they think and speak as we do. No, Rob, you stay right here. Dorbury's got to accept you just as you are."

And Robert stayed. There were those who looked askance at him, and those who could not be reconciled to him, but no one troubled him. As the war drew to a close, and the continued victories of the Union filled the people with enthusiasm, they even began to grow friendly towards him, but he was slow to receive their advances. He was much with Mary and the stream of their love that had been so turbulent, now flowed smoothly and sweetly. Together, they tried to cheer Nannie. "Cheer" is hardly the word either, for she had never lost a certain lightness of spirit that would not let her be entirely cast down. But they tried to bring back the old gayety of her manner that had been her chief charm. She was now back and forth between the Waters' and her own home, and was full of the sweetness of good words and good works on every hand. She was called " Little Miss Nannie," and men had already begun to pay to her that delicate deference which is given to a woman who will never marry. She was always, and would always be " Miss Nannie."

"I wish, Nannie," Mary said to her one day, "that I could give you a part of my happiness." Nannie laughed.

"You poor child," she said, " don't you know that I am very happy. I am happier than any one could ever imagine. I have a lover who will always be young and a love that cannot grow cold. Don't worry about me, I am blest beyond most women."

So they let her go her way and their hearts ceased to ache for her as they saw how cheerful she grew with the joy of doing good. So Nannie began, and so she went on through the years until the end, like a fair flower dying away in its own perfume. There was no selfishness in her subdued sweetness, for when the soldiers came back no one was dearer to them than their dead captain's sweetheart.

The horror of the war has been written of, the broken homes and the broken hearts, but many a life was made sweeter for the fiery trial through which it passed. Stephen Van Doren was stern and implacable until the end. Robert was with him when the news of the surrender came. A shiver passed over his body as if he himself. were the Confederacy which was dying. Then he took his son's hand, and said with a smile, "Well, a principle has been tested and failed. We must submit to the inevitable. From now on—it is the Union," and he opened his window to hear the bells and whistles that proclaimed the people's rejoicings.

The war was ended, but there were gaping wounds to bind up and deep sores that needed careful nursing. The country had been drenched with fraternal blood and the stench of it was an ill savor in the nostrils of both North and South. Grant was a hero, but men were asking, "What is McClellan?" The homecoming soldiers, worn and weary with the long campaign, were being dropped along the wayside from every train. Some homes were hung with evergreens for gladness and others were draped with cypress for those who would never come back. Dorbury had its share of joy and grief. There were returns and there were messages from those who would not return; from lovers, husbands, fathers and brothers. But above the note of sadness was one of joy, for joy is more persistent than grief, if shorter lived.

A little after Appomattox, Robert and Mary were married and went to live in a little home of their own where the two fathers were destined to come many an evening thereafter to fight over the war, talk politics and wrangle as heartily as ever.

Down in Virginia wounded and broken and sore, her heart bleeding for her lost cause and her lost sons; her fields devastated, and her resources depleted, a solemn tone characterized the thanksgiving for the war's end. Walter Stewart thanked God for the triumph of the Union, but wept for the grief of his state. Just about the time that Robert and Mary were united, he and Dolly were married in the little vine-covered church by the rector who had looked askance at him a few years before.

And they were happy with the happiness of youth. Nelson Etheridge had come back safe. Dr. Daniel, now with a major's stripes, walked much in the garden with Emily, from whom, before going away, he had gained a certain promise.

Stewart had indeed come to his own again, and he would have been a delight to his father's eyes could the old colonel have seen him riding about the plantation among the negroes who remained, and directing the repair of the damages which the war had made. He would never go back to Dorbury now, but his memory oft reverted to the old scenes and old acquaintances. His description of Nigger Ed had so pleased Dolly that it resulted in the receipt of the following letter by that gentleman one day in Dorbury:

"My Dear Ed:—You will remember me as one of the boys who used to run around the streets after you years ago, and later as one of the First, *when you were in command*. If you will come down here where there are lots of your people, I'll give you a position on my plantation where you won't be teased. Let me know if you will come. It will be much better than going about ringing an old bell.
"Walter Stewart."

With this letter the negro marched into the office of one of Dorbury's young lawyers one day. The lawyer had been with the First.

"I want you to read dis an' answeh it, mistah —'scuse me—lootenant."

The young fellow took it and his face flushed as he read it.

"Uh huh," said Ed, "now you answer it, please suh."

"All right," the young fellow scribbled for a

moment, and then turned saying, "I think you'd better make it a telegram, Ed."

"Wha' fu'?"

"Shorter, more expressive."

"Les' hyeah it."

The young man picked up the slip of paper and read slowly and carefully, "Mr. Walter Stewart, Stewart House, Rockford Co., Virginia. You be damned."

Ed started as if he had been shot, and then said hastily, "Oh, no, lootenant. I reckon I won't send dat. A telegram's too 'spressive."

"How dare he send for you?" the young man broke in. "You belong to Dorbury. You're a part of it."

"Yes, co'se I is, but I wants to be 'spressive and curtchus too. Jes' you write an' tell him some'p'n 'bout me wanting to 'tain my 'ficial position."

This advice was taken and the result was that Walter threw the household into convulsions over an epistle couched in the most elegant language which informed Mr. Stewart that while he appreciated the very kind offer, the writer—Ed couldn't write a line—preferred to retain his official position, in view of the fact that the emoluments thereof had been materially increased.

And it was true. There were men who had

seen that black man on bloody fields, which were thick with the wounded and dying, and these could not speak of him without tears in their eyes. There were women who begged him to come in and talk to them about their sons who had been left on some Southern field, wives who wanted to hear over again the last words of their loved ones. And so they gave him a place for life and everything he wanted, and from being despised he was much petted and spoiled, for they were all fanatics.

THE END